About the Author

Elizabeth lives in rural Staffordshire, enjoying walking with her husband Terry and being vicar of four churches. Ministry experience includes five years as a mental health chaplain, as well as leading quiet days and helping others in their faith journey. Her degrees in Psychology and Theology add insight to her writing. Elizabeth enjoys knitting and dabbling in art for leisure, as well as recently developing mindfulness and art with spirituality. Her blog is a mix of art, reflections on life, mental health and faith. She has two adult daughters.

Are We There Yet?

A spiritual journey of redemption and recovery from depression to discovering the joy of being me

Elizabeth Jones

Are We There Yet?
A spiritual journey of redemption and
recovery from depression to discovering
the joy of being me

Olympia Publishers
London

www.olympiapublishers.com
OLYMPIA PAPERBACK EDITION

A CIP catalogue record for this title is
available from the British Library.

ISBN: 978-1-80074-251-2

The information in this book has been compiled by way of general
guidance only. Neither the author nor the publisher shall be liable or
responsible for any loss or damage allegedly arising from any
information or suggestion in this book.

First Published in 2022

Olympia Publishers
Tallis House
2 Tallis Street
London
EC4Y 0AB
Printed in Great Britain

Dedication

I dedicate this book to my husband, Terry. I thank God for the gift that he is, for his love, his support and patience. I also dedicate this book to the two women who have supported me, prayed for me and been there for me during this journey: my dear 'big sister' in Christ, Valerie Morris and my spiritual director, who wished to remain anonymous, and sadly died before this book was published. Without them I would not have travelled very far on this long and winding road.

Acknowledgements

I want to thank all my friends who have been supportive – too many to mention individually. Some have walked with me a short way and others were always there, the sort of friends you can rely on to still be there even when we haven't spoken for a while.

I am also grateful to all the people who have led quiet days, retreats and given me counselling. Some counsellors were part of the Lichfield Diocese Listening Ear scheme of six sessions of professional counselling free of charge for clergy and their family. Those responsible for my pastoral care within the diocese (bishops and others) have all been caring and compassionate in their offers of support when I needed it.

Finally, I thank my first husband Ron for the years we shared together, the good times and the bad. He always supported me and encouraged me to develop and extend myself, to go away on retreats and follow the path God called me on. I thank him for letting me go with forgiveness. I also thank my daughters for their love and support.

As a Consultant Psychotherapist for many years, over the decades I have become somewhat familiar with the journeys people make towards emotional wellness from very dark, difficult, life-threatening places.

As I read *Are we there yet?* (alongside her poetry and pictures) I became utterly absorbed and found my heart, hardened by the stories of thousands of patients, was engaged and deeply moved. Here is a woman who has the courage and the sheer talent to make explicit what most people can only begin to utter or imagine.

I believe this work must be taken seriously. It is at once a unique, personal insight into depression and the struggle for recovery, and at the same time it has a universality: it speaks to everyone who has experienced such a struggle, and to those of us who seek to help. Elizabeth combines cartography with art, and the contours she charts are at once recognisable and beautiful.

I cannot recommend it too highly: I feel sure it would find a place not only on the curricula of psychotherapy training institutions but would be recommended to patients and carers as exceptional bibliotherapy.

Judith Miller

Psychotherapist with many years in practice in Central London and New York

ABOUT THIS BOOK

Looking at the swans on the river I think of the cross-stitch sampler I made when I was forty years old. It was a snapshot of my life then, with various important aspects depicted in pictures. This book is like that – not the whole story but a series of snapshots from the album of my life. Most of it is from journal entries I have made over the years.

This book is intended to help –

• People with depression – to give them hope.

• People caring for those with depression – to help them understand both about depression and about the role of faith in recovery.

• Anyone who wants to learn about spiritual growth with a real life example from someone who is fairly average, but happens to have had depression.

Many of the issues faced are common for anyone with or without depression.

The poems and artwork that I refer to are available on my website www.ElizabethJonesDiary.com. It would be too expensive to print them in the book, but I feel they are an integral part of my story and although I describe them here I do suggest that you look at them.

INTRODUCTION

I started this project in the hope that it would help me to reflect upon the journey I've been on for most of my adult life. I hoped that in doing it I would understand more about myself, about the experiences that have made me the person I am today, and gain insight into the interplay between spirituality and recovery from mental illness.

I'm reminded of a line from a song: *"Hello darkness, my old friend, I've come to talk with you again"* (Simon & Garfunkel). Darkness is a good description of depression. People suffering from clinical depression often describe it as a black dog – sometimes big and obvious, sometimes a small but constant companion. My black dog has been of the small variety most of the time and would go missing from time to time, only to come back again and grow big and ferocious. I have had three episodes of being diagnosed as clinically depressed and needing medication. However my spiritual director, whom I have been seeing since 1995 says that in her opinion since then until very recently I had been on the brink of tipping into depression. I hope my story will give a glimpse into what depression can be like. Just as each human being is different, so too, each person's experience of depression will be different. Nevertheless, there are similarities and common threads.

I did this work primarily for myself – for me

For my satisfaction

My insights

My healing and recovery.

A secondary outcome was that it would inform my work as a parish priest and a mental health chaplain.

A third outcome was that others may find it helpful in their journey.

This decision was in itself a step forward in the direction of recovery – taking control and putting myself first (under God). *I am* (and I hesitated to write this in 2011) ***important, I matter.***

The impetus to actually get down to writing this book came as the result of attending a mental health chaplains' annual study conference in 2009. The topic was Recovery. I had completed three weeks of a gradual return to work, and as my colleague and I set off north on our journey, I thought I was OK – tired but OK.

As the conversation turned to church matters as it invariably does when clergy get together. I realised that I was under attack from negative thoughts. I was in a downward spiral of self-doubt and if onlys. If only I was a more charismatic leader, if only I was… all sorts of things, but basically someone else, then the church would be faring better than it was (I was in church half the time and the other half a hospital chaplain). We pulled into the next service station for overpriced coffee, mopping up my tears and helpful conversation.

That evening's speaker was a bipolar sufferer speaking of his and others' experiences of recovery. His main point was that although the literature is all positive about recovery and assumes everyone will get better, the reality isn't quite as rosy. Some people don't 'get better'. With this cheerful thought I retired to bed and when I awoke wrote the following in my journal:

I *am* recovering, but am I getting better? Really well and totally free or is it respite till the next time? Will my life always be overshadowed by depression? That illness that stalks the mind, waiting to bring me down; down into the pit of despair, that place where I don't want to be. But part of me conspires to conjure up those negative thoughts. Once more I wish I were dead: that recurring theme going through my head, weaving itself in and out, entering unbidden into conscious thought. I wish it would go – be gone! Away with you! I want to be well, positive, and glad to be alive. But I'm not. I'm stuck in a rut, going down that familiar track of comparing myself to others and always coming out worse. If only…if only…

"Are we there yet? I wish we were," I asked Granddad on the way to Brighton beach, with its stones that hurt your feet. "You'll wish your life away," he replied. How right he was.

Recovery is a lifelong journey, not the destination. Recovery is the wrong word. There's no going back to my former state. If I did, that wouldn't be progress. I've been depressed on and off for so many years. Is it just my personality? A weakness in me that means I can't handle stress over a certain amount?

My granddad's comment – "You'll wish your life away" has stuck with me. I have very few memories of my early years but this one is informative. We usually went to Brighton for days out and holidays on the beach. I remember travelling in the back of the car, keen to see the first glimpse of sea on the horizon, like most children constantly asking if we were there.

I wasn't enjoying the journey. Perhaps I was travel sick (a complaint I haven't totally grown out of). I clearly didn't want to be where I was.

It's the journey that counts, not arriving, someone once said. They are right. I've spent most of my life living in the past, churning over what happened or what was said or worrying about the future, imagining different scenarios. The lesson I'm learning now is to live in the present moment more. When I started putting this book together I was not well enough to be working full time in ministry. I was suffering from stress and tiredness plus bereavement and depression.

Writing this book helped me to look back through the lens of recovery. Seeing how I'd been helped in the past enabled me to learn and put structures in place in my life. I built on those foundations along with help from other people.

There were times when, as part of my regular prayer time, I used some of the prayers and reflections plus the artwork which I've produced. They are arranged chronologically in a folder and I used them in a cyclical manner, a new one each day. This helped me to continue the benefit I gained when writing them as well as helping me reflect upon how far I had come since they were produced.

The first draft of this book was finished in May 2011. I decided to 'put it to bed' for the time being as I was about to move to a new house, a new church and a new chapter (or is that a new volume?) of life. I would be far too busy to work on this and anyway it felt right to draw a line in the sand and move on emotionally. I decided that I would revisit it (perhaps) and write some theoretical reflection. This happened with a sabbatical in early 2018. I did move on emotionally, continued healing and moved on into good health... but I will let you get to that part of the story rather than spoil the ending now.

In February 2020, whilst considering prayerfully if I really should publish my story with pictures and poems, I painted a flower during a painting and prayerful/mindfulness exercise and composed this whilst out walking a couple of days later.

Are we there yet? Yes, we are! And have been for a while. And now I'm rested, refreshed, recuperated enough and ready to tell you the story of why and how I got to where I am today. Where am I? I am well. I am OK. Most of the time, that is. I have my days of being frazzled round the edges, tired and stressed, but – hey – there's no way I'm depressed! No – I've arrived. I'm here in the land of being well, thanks to my loving Father God, my brother Jesus, and the work of the Holy Spirit within me. I hope that my story will encourage you to continue on your journey of recovery, of taking care of yourself, of letting yourself be loved by God, by others and, most importantly, by yourself. May God bless you as you read my story. May God bless you and make His face to shine upon you and be gracious to you and give you His Peace. Amen.

One thing I've learnt is that I need to enjoy the journey rather than straining to see the sea on the horizon. All journeys have a beginning. The journey of my recovery started around 1984 when I recognised that I needed to be on it.

CHAPTER 1
Initial Diagnosis – The Journey Begins

As a young mother, aged twenty-seven, I went shopping in town as I usually did. We needed apples but when confronted with the choice in the shop I was incapable of making the decision of which to buy, so I went home without any. Walking across the Town Hall square I looked up at the imposing tower of the parish church. I had to admit to myself that my friend's diagnosis that I was depressed may be true. She'd told me one day as I was in tears yet again that I was depressed and should see my doctor. Up until then I had tried to deny it, too scared to go to the doctor's, afraid of the unknown. I called out to God, "Please don't let them take the kids off me."

The doctor diagnosed anxiety and depression which he treated with imipramine for three or four months.

But what about God? Did he hear my cry for help? The children were not taken into care. I was not labelled an inadequate mother. As is often the case, God worked slowly. Like many people I'd had the children christened as babies. I had no great belief in God; it was the thing to do, an excuse for a party to celebrate their birth as well as giving them 'a good start in life'.

The year following my cry for help my eldest daughter was invited to Sunday school as she had just started school. An invitation arrived inviting her to a harvest party, then one for a Christmas event. They were put behind the clock on the mantelpiece but I didn't get around to taking her. One day someone from the church came to visit and invited us personally. I later learnt that the visitor had tried several times without success and this was her last attempt. She told God that if there wasn't a parking space and I wasn't in, then she'd give up. And when she left, she felt the visit had been "a waste of time". I was unresponsive, and didn't even switch the TV off!

However, the seeds had been sown. I discovered that my younger daughter could go in the crèche whilst the elder was in Junior Church and I stayed in the service. It seemed a good idea. The younger child needed company. I was finding her hard work – the terrible twos – and waiting for a place at playgroup, as well as needing speech therapy. So I started to attend the church and gradually realised I did believe. Taking the younger daughter to Toddlers' Church midweek and having other mums to talk with helped too. It can be very isolating being at home with young children and very little adult company.

While the children played, under the supervision of Aunty Brenda, we had a discussion. We then went into the lady chapel for a little service and craft activity. I noticed that the other mums had something I wanted. I sensed a real joy and peace and was fascinated to see that when the curate's wife led us, singing *Sing Hosanna*, children and adults alike sang with gusto. They looked as if they really believed the words they sang. My childhood faith was re-awakened and I started to believe again.

I had been christened as a baby, sent to Sunday school and

confirmed when I was twelve years old. All I can remember is walking from the parish room to the church wearing a white dress and a veil on my head. I did believe and used to have prayer cards stuck on my bedroom mirror. I remember my first disco, at age thirteen, at the local Methodist hall. I danced and sang along to *Spirit in the Sky*, knowing where I would go when I died. But I soon dropped away. Boys and discos were more interesting. And my faith disappeared. By the time I married and had children I had vague ideas of good and evil in the spiritual realm, but not much more than that.

1986 – in the pit of despair

Music has a way of reaching us in a way that words alone don't. I had a tape of praise songs based on the psalms which I found helpful. It's a great way of learning scriptures that build us up, enabling us to put our trust in God. The psalms contain many prayers that can become part of our stock to draw on when our own words fail. However, there was one day that the chorus words "Lord you put a new song in my mouth, a hymn of praise to our God"[1] were stuck in my mind and it was so annoying because I really did not feel like singing a song. I was down in the dumps. Life didn't seem worth living. I eventually looked up the psalm in my Bible and got a real shock. Psalm 40 described my condition – in "the slimy pit… the mud and mire." Wow! God seemed to be saying that He understood, He had heard my cry and He was promising to lift me out. Although "troubles without number surrounded me, my sins have overtaken me… They are more than the hairs of my head and my heart fails within me" the psalm was helping me to acknowledge my need and ask God to help and to put my trust in Him.

There was also a section about telling what God has done in the great congregation, that I felt had something to do with me but I wasn't sure why, so I circled it. I later felt that it was the first call to a ministry of preaching.

God is my Daddy.

My first drawing, done in April 1988, was an image of me as a young girl skipping along a road towards a light. I'd written "God is my daddy and he keeps me safe as I skip towards him. He lights my way and loves me on my journey… Lord, give me Christ-like qualities, so that your light will shine through me in the work I have to do for you. Amen."

I was learning to trust God as I embarked on this journey of discipleship. It was also the year that I made a major leap of faith and trust in Jesus. I attended several March for Jesus events, one of which was at the NEC. I went with some people from church and was introduced to a vicar's wife who had just moved into the area. During the time of worship, we sang *Such Love,*[2] which touched my heart, as I realised at a deeper level that Jesus really did love me and died for me to bring me healing. However, there was a point in the worship when I was unable to raise my hands as others were – not out of embarrassment but because I felt unable to worship. Something was stopping me. As I cried, I could see my husband's face. The newly introduced vicar's wife asked what was wrong and I told her I didn't know, just that I couldn't worship. She said, "It's your husband, isn't it?" How did she know? It was the first time I had experienced someone having a word of knowledge. I told her that yes, I could see his face. She prayed for me – I don't remember what she said. However, I do remember imagining that I was offering him up to God in the same way that Abraham offered up Isaac as a sacrifice.

My relationship with my husband had been 'rocky'. The more keen I became as a Christian, the more anti-church he was. I felt that if pushed, I would choose Jesus rather than him. The year prior to this, on my 30th birthday, I was in tears, saying my marriage was over. I couldn't continue. But as a Christian wife I felt I couldn't leave him. Back in the 1960s and 70s while I was growing up divorce was very unusual. I knew only one person whose parents were divorced. There was more societal pressure to keep a marriage going rather than ending it. I couldn't and wouldn't take that step of ending it. So I prayed that he would leave me. He stayed. Things got worse. So I'm not sure how much of a 'sacrifice' offering him to God was. It may have been more of a case of "I don't want him, you have him".

We had started courting when I was fifteen and I knew my parents didn't approve. He was part of my teenage rebellion. Nevertheless, I fell in love with him, and our relationship deepened and became sexual while I was still fifteen. I had committed myself to him totally. When we got married, we had been living together for some months and I couldn't go to the vicar and ask for a church wedding. I couldn't give a false address and I couldn't admit to living in sin. I couldn't lie to a priest. I didn't believe in God and felt a hypocrite to consider a church wedding. I didn't believe I deserved a white dress and anyway white doesn't suit me. We lived opposite the Methodist chapel, but I discounted that as not being a proper church. (As I wrote this, I was a Resident Minister of an Anglican/Methodist Local Ecumenical Partnership! – God has such a sense of humour!) So, the registry office it was on 4th June 1977, with the photos showing the bunting out for the

Queen's Silver Jubilee and St Paul's church in the background.

As I got to know the deaconess, Valerie, (it was she who had visited me) and trusted her enough to talk to her about my past and the things that worried me, various issues surfaced and she prayed for me. God started on the inner work; including my guilt at becoming sexually active so young, thinking I was pregnant but wasn't, and that I had been raped by a stranger. I confessed these things and prayed for forgiveness for the part I played in them. I regretted not having the big white church wedding. I can remember sitting on the desk at school singing "We're going to the chapel and we're gonna get married, going to the Chapel of Love". I *knew* he was the one for me and one of the desires of my heart was to marry him, in church.

Scriptures can be life giving, but they can also be used to keep people in unhealthy situations, e.g. the instructions to wives are often used to keep women in submission. I tried to submit to my husband. I wouldn't leave him, even though I was unhappy, because I thought it was wrong to do so. Whatever my inner motivations of handing over my husband to God, things did change in quite a remarkable way as I trusted God more and put Jesus first. Things came to a head and we didn't speak from one Friday to a Sunday and I thought it was all over. How wrong I was! My prayers were answered and my husband became a Christian on Pentecost Sunday 1989 in a very sudden and dramatic conversion experience. We re-made our marriage vows in church on 20th August 1989. I would love to say "and they all lived happily ever after" but this is real life and not a fairy story.

CHAPTER 2
Learning to be Still

A Parish Retreat at Shallowford House in Spring 1990 was a new experience for me in which I learnt about a different way of prayer. We were told to go for a walk and look around us and let the surroundings 'speak' to us. I enjoy this type of prayer and often find God speaking to me through what I can see.

That day I heard the invitation to "Be still and know that I am God" (Psalm 46:10). It's one that I receive on a regular basis. I needed to become calm, to still the negative voices and distractions. Walking and looking at the hedgerows, the hills etc. is one way of doing this. To really take notice of the details can simultaneously draw attention away from oneself and be open to reflect more deeply about oneself.

That day as I walked along a lane and picked a hawthorn in flower, I became aware at a deeper level, of God's love and His acceptance of me as I am. As I considered the hedgerows, I felt thankful to God for them. I considered the difference between the fairly ordinary hawthorn and the more elegant and popular rose. If I were to be a flower, I would rather be a beautiful rose than an ordinary flower in the hedgerow. However, as I thanked God for the hawthorns, I realised that it was just as beautiful as a rose, but different, and that I should be glad that God made me to be me. I felt that God was saying that He loves me as I am and it didn't matter whether I was thorn or rose. He made me to be me and that I should be still and know that He loves me.

It was also the first step of me accepting and valuing myself as I am and not wishing I were someone else. At the time I was not aware of how deep my self-hatred went. I was still at surface level of appearances. It took over twenty years for me to be able to say that "I like myself and am glad I am me". There have been glimpses of it on the way, but they haven't lasted.

I got stuck into church life, attending Bible study/fellowship groups and eventually did the Bishop's Certificate Course. At the end of that we had to consider what next? I had been helped so much by Valerie and I wanted to help other people in the way that I had. I wanted to tell people all about Jesus and how faith can help. Someone said I should be a Lay Reader. What's one of those, I asked? I learnt that a Lay Reader is a minister who is not ordained, takes services and preaches. They are now known as Readers. So the next step was to prepare for that. I got through the selection process. For me, it was my way of being able to fulfil that call to tell others that I'd read in Psalm 40.

There were other pointers towards being a priest, but remember that was back in the days before women were ordained; and I didn't even know it was being discussed, despite being on the church council. It didn't get talked about. I just assumed that only men were ordained. So being a Reader was my way of being a priest.

One of the other pointers to ordination that I felt was from God, was when Valerie had been praying for me and she felt that God wanted me to read some of Zechariah Chapter 3. She had been listening to my problems and difficulties. I had been bringing to God, through her, all my sins and the baggage of my past that I wanted to put behind me. The section of Zechariah focussed on the cleansing of sin. However, for me the bit that stuck out, was that he was a priest, and the line about having a place in governing God's house. I didn't understand why, but I just knew it was important and had something to do with me.

May 1991 – retreat at All Stretton

This was my first attempt at a retreat. I spent Tuesday to Thursday in the ground floor flat of a friend's house so, although I was on my own, she was never far away. My hope at the start was that God would speak to me and that I would be able to respond. During my time I reflected upon the world: that God had created it, and also that I was known and chosen before I was even conceived. These great theological themes are still beyond my intellect. They go deep to the heart and call forth a response of trust and hope. During the retreat I detected a lack of trust on my part, and a desire to trust more. Security and feeling safe are important to mental health and an increase of this can be obtained through the Christian faith. One image that has become important to me over the years is that of being held in the shadow of God's wings – and I drew a picture of me being enveloped by huge wings with the glow of God's love also surrounding me.

During this retreat God seemed to be telling me to be still. I'm an activist, I don't 'do' being still very easily. This has been a hard lesson for me to learn through my Christian journey and a skill that takes patience to develop. However, the practice of being still in God's presence is one that pays dividends.

At the end of the retreat, I felt that I'd drawn closer to God but was very aware, and frustrated by, my inability to accept His love and to love Him in return.

Ten days before this retreat I had written Jesus a letter concerning a miscarriage I'd had in November the previous year. In it I thanked Jesus for the ministry of David who had prayed for me and said he had had a 'picture' of Jesus holding a baby girl. He felt that God was saying she was mine and with Him. One of the pains I felt after the miscarriage was that I wouldn't hold my baby. This time of prayer was healing that wound and the letter was my response. In the letter I thanked Jesus for the healing tears which soothed my wounds, for taking care of my daughter, and for holding her safe. I asked what her name is, and liked to think it was Joy. I was glad she was with Jesus and accepted that the pregnancy wasn't to be. In those days people didn't have funerals or prayer for a miscarriage; it was simply disposed of like a heavy period.

The letter went on to ask Jesus to help me 'let go', to show me what stops me from total commitment, to release me from the chains that bind me, the worry of what others will think of me. This retreat was the first of many where Jesus gradually undid the many chains that have bound me over the years.

As I meditated on Psalm 33, I slightly changed the psalm's words to express how joyful I felt, and my trust in His plans for me. As I went for a walk in the hills, I compared walking in the hills with the Christian journey. There's never a dull moment. (At least not many!) And I wonder, what's next along the Way? Rough or smooth, with eyes fixed on Jesus, it hardly matters. But look away from Him and it's easy to stray. I have often felt frustration, anguish and pain, with the scorching heat of God's all-seeing eyes meeting me. Nothing is hidden from God. I hide from myself but He sees everything. He sees my shame and pain, and I believe He cries for me. His healing tears drop down into my soul: cleansing, refreshing and healing. Peace, contentment and joy are there in the resting places, the cool, refreshing oasis. It would be easy to stay sheltered out of the wind and rain but to reach the journey's end I have to endure some pain. And so, I slowly regain strength and peace, feeling battered but secure in the knowledge of God's love I'm ready to join the Way again. Some of the best views are to be gained from difficult routes. A stick helps tired legs and clears away thorns but only if it's used. On the Way, God's Word will be my staff. I know He has the words of life and I ask God to give me enough faith to act on them, to believe and use them. I concluded that Jesus is the provider of all and that He wants me to make this journey. So I asked Him to provide me with all I need, for on my own I can go nowhere and it's dull every moment without Him. I prayed for God's help to keep me going with Him, to keep me on the right path and never stray too far. But that when I do, He would bring me back to the right path.

May 1991

I was learning that I could rely on God and lean on Him in difficult times. I was also thinking about the way that I often looked for God in various places: church, books, charismatic prayer meetings and songs, praying with other people, as well as being aware of His presence in the beauty of the countryside and nature. One day whilst listening to a song version of Psalm 91 I imagined myself being held in God's wings and did a drawing of this image, along with the verses that I felt speak

31

to me. I was warm and safe. The verses that particularly stood out for me were:

Verse 2: He is my refuge, and my fortress, my God in whom I trust.

Verse 4: He will cover you with his feathers, and under his wings you will find refuge; his faithfulness will be your shield and rampart.

Verse 11: For he will command his angels concerning you to guard you in all your ways.

Verses 14–16 (I changed it from masculine to feminine pronouns)

"Because she loves me," says the Lord, "I will rescue her; I will protect her, for she acknowledges my name. She will call on me, and I will answer her; I will be with her in trouble, I will deliver her and honour her. With long life I will satisfy her and show her my salvation."

CHAPTER 3
Stress Increases But God Is With Me

Autumn 1992 was a busy time for me. I was getting more involved in church with a Thursday evening bible study/fellowship group, organising the church 'orchestra', learning to play piano, and helping at the drop-in we ran. Then there was the YMCA furniture project which I administered, plus playing in the Tutbury Band and a clarinet quartet. On top of all that 'leisure' activity, I was running a household and working part-time as a teacher. One of the things I have learnt over the years is that I react to stress by becoming depressed. At the end of November, I wrote in my journal that I was finding it difficult to cope with stress and being busy, asking myself if I was doing too much, and if so, what should go? I felt God saying that He would direct me.

On 1st December I was depressed, didn't want to praise God, even though I believed it would 'release' me. I thought I didn't deserve release, I deserved to suffer. The tension was showing itself in my relationship with my husband, but I felt I shouldn't bother anyone else with it—Valerie had enough on her plate.

On the 2nd I felt far from God. I had eaten too much chocolate the day before and wondered why I still did it. Depressed, but not as much as in the past, I found it difficult to concentrate on prayer. Isaiah 49 says that the Lord will not forget Israel. I wondered if the same went for me. Am I engraved on the palm of his hand? Yet verse 23 says, "I am the Lord; those who hope in me will not be disappointed." So I put my hope in Him, and I was not disappointed as this is what I thought he was saying to me:

"Yes, Liz, I love you. You are precious to me and always in my sight. I watch over you like a father his newborn babe. I adore you. I am proud of you and of all you do in my name. Yes, Liz, I love you. Do not doubt it. Whatever happens I will be there to guide and comfort you. Do not be distressed when hard times come. They are the refiner's fire. I'm proving you, making you truly mine. There are things you do not know now which I will reveal to you. Do not be afraid. All in my own time will be revealed. I love you, Liz. Believe me. I do. Do not doubt it. Do not make me sad by rejecting it. Accept my love."

This difficulty accepting love – how do I overcome it? What is the answer to this frustration? The answer I felt God give was, "Sing more spiritual songs, use the gift of tongues and melody to lift your spirit towards me. It doesn't matter if your mind isn't 'with it' – it will be brought into line by your spirit as you give way to the Holy Spirit within you."

Writing this at the end of a thirty-two-year-old marriage that I know had been difficult on and off for well over twenty-five years, I wonder what kept me going. Prayer and determination played a part, as did a sense of doing what is right. However, a big player in it was God – or what I thought God was saying to me. I may be wrong. It may be that I was projecting my inner thoughts onto God. Or I may be right. God may have been speaking to my inner being; to bring me through to a time when ending the marriage was right for both of us.

On 9th Dec I thought God said to me, "You are long suffering and patient. I am healing you and him. Be patient. There is fault on both sides. But I am the Lord your God and there is nothing I cannot do. So be patient. I am healing you both and making you whole. You do love him. I see deep inside you and in there is a great love for him that has been hurt and is frightened. I will bring it out slowly and gently. Relax in me. Direct your love to me and don't worry about him for I love him for you. I have enough love for you all. Unlike a human parent I can take your love and give it to him so he will not feel unloved. So love me in his place. I know you don't understand. Trust and obey. I will not disown you or let you down."

January 1993

Like many people I found Christmas a strain, being cooped up in the house with the family. As well as this I was due to start training as a Lay Reader in January. I felt anxious and depressed about this, but put my trust in God and had peace that it was the right thing to be doing. However, negative voices persisted in my mind. I wanted to praise God and wondered why I was so down. I knew God had done great things, that thanks to Jesus all my sins were forgiven. Although I wanted to be glad and worship God with all my being, I couldn't. And yet, I was determined to reject the negative thoughts in Jesus' name and praise the Lord, my Redeemer, my God, my all.

23 March 1993 – Parish quiet day

Although I wrote in my journal that I was disappointed that I couldn't get into the meditation on Isaiah 43:1–8, I did manage to write a poem as I realised that God has been with me always, through good and bad and that he will take my restlessness and turn it into rest. These verses from Isaiah have been special to me since I had a miscarriage and the lady from church who visited me brought a plant with a card with the first couple of verses in it. I do not believe that God sends us difficulties and suffering to test us, but I do believe that when they do, He does sustain us and our faith is tested. And with that testing our faith (and by that, I mean trust) in God is strengthened and deepened.

I was learning to "Be still and know that I am God". I was learning that God cares for me, He made me and delights in me. He wants me to come to Him and be still. He has called me by name and I am His. He has brought me through many waters and will carry me through more. There is no need for me to fear because He is with me. So, although I didn't know where He was leading me, all I needed to do was trust Him and obey and let Him lead me into fullness of life. In Him are my peace and security.

By October that year though I had let my prayer life slip. The pressures of work and my mother's illness (breast cancer and secondary in spine) had led to my over-eating and feeling low. I thought the root may be pride and low self-esteem. On 1st November 1993 my mother died. The funeral and cremation were on 5th November. My husband went to Relate, for his first counselling session that morning. I later joined him for sessions too. They helped us with communication.

CHAPTER 4
Going Deeper In Prayer: Who Am I?

In December 1993 as I was meditating on Jeremiah 18:1–6 (the passage about God as a potter), I imagined having a conversation with God, the potter who takes pride in his work. It's his clay to do with as he wishes.

GOD SAYS: Does a piece of clay own itself? Do you own yourself? Did you not give yourself to me as I gave my son to you on Calvary? You no longer own yourself. I own you. You are my clay and I will model you as I wish.

I REPLY: Holy Spirit, help me to give myself totally into the potter's hands. I don't want to be me. But do I want to be what you want me to be? I want to be someone I like. I don't like the way I go along doing what's expected and right, always dotting the I's and crossing the T's and getting the apostrophe in the right place. And don't make a spelling mistake! Do I want to be so precise? No! I would rather be creative than objective and correct. I want to be sure of what I believe and to be brave enough to stand up and be counted.

I don't like me. Me is selfish, insecure and wants to be right. I don't like me. I want to change into a better me. A me, I will like and approve. Lord, help me to move. Help me to move my position, away from looking at myself with loathing to a place where I can say, "I'm OK – God made me – and I'm good." Right now, my position is uncomfortable.

I don't like me but I'm frightened to allow you into change me, to break me, mould me and renew me. A part of me won't budge – it's scared; scared of the possible outcome. If you look too close, if you go right in, you might see what I see – the me that I keep hidden. And you might not like the hidden me. You might look and say "Yuk" and then discard me, leave me, desert me, alone in the dark.

I have come to the end. Or rather, a crossroads. Do I turn back – or go forward? If I go forward – which way? Through my fears and tears I cannot see. So, Holy Spirit, guide me. Into your hands I give myself. Show me how to trust completely, unreservedly, totally. I do really want to be remoulded – I'm just scared!

GOD'S REPLY: You can be artistic, creative <u>and</u> precise. Paying attention to detail and getting things right, that's my way of doing things. Look at my creation. It's not shoddy or quickly thrown together with no regard for detail. Don't belittle what I have made you. I have made you the way you are. Rejoice and be glad. Be positive, not negative. I am moulding you. Trust me. Keep on with me. As your insecurity goes and you become more secure in me, then you will see more clearly the person you are meant to be. And you <u>will</u> like you because <u>I only make good things</u>.

I came to the conclusion that I needed to spend more time with God, that I had become dry. Clay needs to be wet to remain workable. If I am to minister to others, I need to keep my own spiritual reserves topped up. If I were running a soup kitchen, I'd have to go to the shops to buy ingredients or the soup and bread. If I am to give spiritual food, I need to have enough to give.

A sign of the way that God has continued to work in me

and the healing I've experienced, is that when I was using this meditation in February 2010, I realised it was no longer me. I didn't feel that way about myself. I now like me and am glad to be me. I had started to paint and was learning to draw. I had changed.

23 June 1994 – Parish quiet day at St Francis', Greystones

I've had a difficult relationship with food over the years. My weight has gone up and down like a yo-yo. I have turned to food for comfort and out of boredom. Although I knew that I turned to food for the wrong reasons, I had very little self-control to overcome it. It was almost as if the food – or something inside me – had a hold on me. There was also a period when I had a tendency to self-medicate on alcohol, wanting to use it to block out reality, to feel better. I think that if I hadn't been fortunate enough to have had the support and opportunities for retreats and healing that I have had, plus the fear of the shame of discovery for someone in my position, then I may well have become alcoholic.

On this quiet day I also pondered who I am, what I'm here for, and who I am when I'm not serving a purpose for someone else. I was beginning to recognise that I felt trapped by my various roles, making myself busy with them to avoid being just me.

I often find walking and praying helpful. I go for a walk with God. It helps me to ponder things in my mind with Him. It also means that external things and events are able to trigger thoughts – possibly interpreted as messages from God. A month after that quiet day I went for such a prayer walk and noted in my journal that I'd seen a woman at a window of her house and imagined she was being held in prison. She could go out if she turned round and went through the door. This led me to wonder if I am looking out, waiting to escape. If so, who is the jailor? Who holds the key? God or me? Is God my jailor, or do I hold myself ransom? I concluded that God is there to free the captives – I am my own jailor. The jail in question was my marriage.

My first individually guided retreat: it's OK to be mad at God
In October 1994 I went on an individually guided retreat at a Franciscan house. I was to spend five days in silence, except for a daily meeting with my guide for about an hour and joining in the morning, midday and evening prayer times with the others in the house. My agenda was to seek God's guidance about whether or not He was calling me for ordination. His agenda was rather different.

In this safe place I was able to overcome my fears that God wouldn't speak to me, would ignore me, or I wouldn't be able to hear him. I was scared – like a small fury animal in a cage running round its wheel and avoiding being picked up. By the second full day I was aware of much pain and hurt, fear and feelings of failure and rejection that had been pushed down inside. I wrote a letter to God, which was very helpful in letting out anger about my mum's death. When I went for a walk, I felt that God was walking with me and that He would be a mother and a father to me. I felt as though He was walking next to me, with his arm around my shoulders. Two songs became important too – *Be bold, be strong*[3] and *Be still for the presence of the Lord.*[4] Singing songs which are based on scripture is a good way of letting those positive, affirming, words sink in deep. It builds trust in God and allows the healing process to happen.

Art can also be therapeutic. When walking through a wood I saw a stagnant pond and a running brook. I drew them when I got back as they had spoken to me. I felt God saying that I wouldn't be like the stagnant pond, but that God's spirit would flow through me, clearing away the debris.

I also read the story of the prodigal son and made connections with my own life. I made a cartoon strip of it, as if it were to be published in a paper. The title is "CELEBRATE AND BE GLAD – Liz was dead and is alive again; she was lost and is found." There's a notice too reading "God is proud to announce the safe return of LIZ much loved daughter".

I ended the retreat feeling joyful and peaceful; aware that God is with me and concluding that the more I accept myself, the more I'll be close to Jesus, and it has been that way.

Names are important. Who am I?

Elizabeth Jane Carter is on my birth certificate. As a young child I was Bess then Liz and only Elizabeth when in trouble or on 'Sunday best'. In June 1977 I became Elizabeth Jane Fairless and then simply Mum or being Fran's mum and Steph's mum.

In December 1994 I had some counselling with a Christian who used transactional analysis techniques and asked me to imagine Jesus sitting in the corner of the room. We worked with the two parts of me, Liz and Elizabeth, who became aware of each other and were reconciled. "Elizabeth" had been dominating me (my inner parent) and I wanted "Liz" to be allowed out more (my inner child).

Over the years I've referred to 'parent' as Elizabeth, 'adult' as Liz and 'child' as Bess. I've become more at peace with the various aspects of my personality; and by the time I started writing this book I had started to even like being called Elizabeth. By the time I had finished writing, I am not just happy to be called Elizabeth, but find it brings a sense of being loved and special with it.

In December 1994 I was licensed as a Reader. It was shortly before that, when we were at one of the training events at Shallowford House, gathered round the coffee trolley I noticed that one of our number was missing. Where was she? She had changed tracks and was going to be ordained!!!! A stab in the heart – if she can, then why can't I?

Learning different ways of praying with a Spiritual Director

I had been intrigued by a friend who was a Third Order Franciscan and talked of her spiritual director. I thought it would be good for me to have someone to talk over where I was with my journey of faith and also to help me explore whether I was indeed being called to ordination. So I was introduced to someone who has helped me enormously.

She has helped me grow by not directing me in a 'thou shalt do this or that' way, rather she has accompanied me. In the safe space she creates, I am able to tell her things I've told no one else. I've experienced unconditional love – the love I know God has for me. I know that whatever I tell her, she still accepts me, she still wants to see me and she wants the best for me, even when it's painful. There's something about the dynamic of talking with another person – talking therapy – that is not there when you are on your own. All you are doing is saying the words that you are thinking, but by letting them out in the open, they become more real. And often I don't know what I'm thinking until I speak!

My spiritual director has introduced me to different ways

of praying, helped me to discern the direction I should be taking in life, including ministry. She has also heard my confession, said the words of absolution and I've felt the release of the burden of sin (those things which get between me and God). The first time I did this, it was those issues that I had talked and prayed about before with Valerie when God first started to work in me. I knew in my head I was forgiven, but the guilt was still there, lingering in my mind. It was as if the rubbish was in the bin bag but had been left by the back door and getting smelly. The words of absolution enabled my inner self to put the bag in the bin and for it to be taken away. At the time I didn't really understand the theology, but I do know that at a spiritual level something was released and healed. The penance she gave me was to read and pray through *And Can It Be*? This has become one of my favourite hymns, especially the two verses about being imprisoned in sin and the chains falling off and then being able to rise and follow Him. No condemnation now, but clothed in righteousness I am able to approach God's throne, through Christ.

July 1995 – retreat weekend at All Stretton

BE STILL AND KNOW THAT I AM GOD: this is easier said than done. I went for a walk up the valley and wondered if God was really there. Did He care that I thought He may just be in my imagination, a bit of an hallucination? It's just not fair! God has often said "Be still" but on this occasion as I strolled up the hill, admired the view, watched a wandering ewe and was very still, God wasn't there. No matter how I'd stare, I couldn't see Him, I couldn't hear Him, He just wasn't there. Deafened by the silence of his absence, blinded by creation I was left with just one question: why don't I know

God's presence?

This four-day retreat was a time of confronting my inability to stop trying and just relax. My life was dominated by 'oughts' and 'shoulds'. A friend refers to this as a "hardening of the oughteries" and just as deadly as hardening of the arteries. However, I did end the time away feeling peaceful and hopeful for the future, whatever that might be.

August 1995 – a walk in the park

As I went for a walk in the park one day, I sat for a while beneath the spreading branches of a tree, resting in the shade, protected from the sun's burning rays. Looking up all I could see was the undersides of the leaves: dull, uninteresting. Dead against the glittering glimpses of light playing in the gaps, dancing as the breeze blows through the branches. As I looked further, beyond the tree, I caught a glimpse of light, dazzling, free, twinkling like diamonds on the other trees. I wondered if I were hiding under branches, away from Jesus. I glimpse him through the armour and then he's gone. But I long for him, there's a yearning strong within to be with him, resting in the warmth of his love. All I see of me is the dull, underside of the leaf. Do others really see me, like I see the other tree: alive and shining, reflecting the son's light? I didn't think so.

CHAPTER 5
Preparing for Ministry
(but not how I thought I would)

During Lent 1996, I used this Ignatian prayer as I prepared to offer myself for ordination:

Take Lord and receive, all my liberty, my memory, my understanding and my entire will. All that I have and call my own, you have given it all to me. To you, Lord, I return it, everything is yours. Do with it what you will. Give me only your love and your grace. That is enough for me.[5]

It was a period of learning to be still in God's presence and simply offer myself – all the various aspects of my life and who I am – to Him.

After Easter I went to Spring Harvest (a large Christian event held at Butlin's camp) with a group from church. I became aware that I had a tendency to compartmentalise my life, am self-conscious and bothered by what other people think of me. Low self-esteem was an ongoing battle. As part of the preparation for selection for ordination I had to write my life story. This was the first time I'd been asked to reflect on my life and it left me feeling depressed, frustrated in my prayer times and feeling I'd be better off dead.

During a meditation on the raising of Lazarus, when Jesus called me out, nothing happened. I concluded that the prayer time was "pointless, stupid, frustrating" in large capital letters and marks with my pen which had ripped the pages of my journal. "God's not speaking, feel like a hypocrite, might as well forget the whole thing and jump off a cliff." I also felt guilty that I'd finished before the appointed half hour of prayer. I now know that this getting stuck is a sign of something within needing attention. In later years, meditations of Lazarus have been times of healing.

3 May 1996 – from journal of daily prayer, using the collect for Easter 4. "A peaceful session. God will use my experiences and healing of them. I think I will probably be involved in pastoral care. Walking with others the way I have been. This feels right.

Loving with the love that flows through me in Jesus' name, with Jesus as my guide, I will guide; with Jesus as my healer, I will heal; with Jesus as my lover, I will love; with Jesus as my restorer, I will restore. All for the love and glory of God the Father. Amen. So be it, in the power of the Spirit."

1997 – Life begins at forty (or so they say) but for me it felt like a death.

I was going to reach the age of forty in July 1997 and had a sense of my life changing. I started a cross-stitch sampler of my life which was to contain the words LIFE BEGINS AT FORTY – but I didn't finish it until a further five years had elapsed and without that phrase.

The time was right for me to offer myself for ordination within the Church of England. I had been seeing a director of ordinands from the Lichfield Diocese for a couple of years, and we both felt that it was time for me to attend the national selection panel. The national selection panel interviews candidates and give them tasks over a two-day conference. They then either recommend a person goes on to be trained for ordained ministry, or not, to their diocesan bishop. In my times of prayer, I had given away to God my right to choose what I do and aware that I am called by name, honoured and precious and that God loves me (Isaiah 43). Although I thought I was open to the idea of not being ordained, I knew that my time of teaching was coming to an end. I'd had enough of classroom battles with children who didn't want to learn, having been a part-time instructor of typing and office studies at a secondary school for thirteen years.

The selectors did not recommend me. I felt as though my future had been snatched away from me. However, I picked myself up, dusted myself off and knocked on the door of Derby University. I'd been looking forward to the opportunity to study during ordination training, especially the idea that I could study for two years, be ordained and continue to work towards a degree during my curacy.

One of my regrets had been not going to university. My brother was the clever one who went to the grammar school. It was secondary modern for me, with the career's advice being, "office, shop or factory?" There was no way I was going to stay on at school any longer than I had to. I'd already done an extra year, staying on to sixteen, to take CSEs. I refused to go the grammar school for O levels but did agree to a one-year secretarial course at the Tech College: I wanted to get out and earn some money.

My first job had been at the Co-op Insurance on the Life Assurance desk. It's funny that my final job is another type of Life Assurance. I had continued with part-time courses and become a highly qualified secretary. There was an opening to teach, as a part-time instructor at the secondary school I had attended as a child. I taught typing, office studies and in time word processing, spreadsheets and database. The hours suited me with school-aged children. Once I'd started teaching, and realised I had some talent for it, one of the other teachers advised me that if I wanted to eventually become qualified, I'd need A levels and that psychology and sociology would be useful. I'd therefore taken these at night school. Whenever I'd thought about taking a degree via the Open University, I'd not been able to decide on a subject I felt sufficiently interested in. However, now I was standing at a crossroads in life – which way now? The road to ordination had a NO ENTRY sign – perhaps I could train as a counsellor? I didn't fancy being a social worker and definitely didn't want to teach. So, keeping my options as open as possible, and taking advantage of the subjects I already knew something of, I enrolled on a combined subject degree in psychology, sociology and religious studies. After the first year I dropped the sociology and majored in psychology, reasoning that if I were to go down the route of counselling that would be of more use. I chose religious studies because as a Reader I had already a fair amount of knowledge. However as soon as I started to study, I realised how much more there was to learn.

It was so wonderful after the wounding experience of 'rejection' by the church to be welcomed with open arms by the university. It was a strange experience to study the Christian faith alongside other faiths on an equal playing field. I was also angry with the church – and wondering what God was playing at, if indeed there was a God. I didn't lose my faith, but rather than standing firm on the rock I was, at times, clinging on by my fingernails. I didn't keep much of a journal during this time as I was busy with university work.

In January 1999 I had a wonderful field trip to India as part of an Interfaith Dialogue module. It was also an opportunity for God to speak into the darkness. We were in a temple on the southernmost tip of the subcontinent. When we entered, I'd taken off my sunglasses to be able to see but had left my normal ones on the bus. When we entered the room with a plinth and 'Om' figure I followed the example of the others and knelt down. I wasn't worshipping it, but I was wondering where God was, IF God was.

The 'Om' was out of focus and reminded me of a foetus. I felt God say "Stay connected to me. Even though you are unaware of it, like a baby is fed by a mother, so I will continue to feed you." God was holding onto me in this spiritual wilderness.

In May that year I had a head-on car crash. I came out of it badly bruised but with nothing broken, thanks to the seat belt and air bag. The police officer who visited me the next day said he didn't think they'd get anyone out of my car alive! It was just before my exams, which I was determined to still take. So my GP put me on some antidepressants to get me through. I needed them – when I eventually got to see a psychologist for the report required by the insurance claim, I was one tick short of having post-traumatic stress. The GP said I'd only need to be on medication for about three months so in September I came off them. What I didn't realise was that this should be done gradually! I crashed into deep depression. So once more I was given antidepressants. However, I am glad this happened because when I was ill I had flashbacks of the car accident overlaying onto the trauma of being raped in my teenage years. I was then able to get professional counselling for that, which was a big step forward in healing for me.

Those born since the 1980s will view sex differently to those of us who are of an earlier era. I was a teenager in the 1970s. Our parents and authority figures were not of the swinging sixties era. Back then, good girls did not have sex before they were married and they certainly didn't start sexual relationships under the age of sixteen (which is still the legal age of consent). At least that was what we believed was correct and those who did allow a boy to go further than he should felt they were being daring and breaking the rules. It was very unusual to live together before getting married, which was referred to as 'living in sin'. This is why my starting a sexual relationship at only fifteen left a deep mark of shame and guilt. This was compounded when I was raped. I had buried the rape and forgotten about it until God brought it to the surface as something to be dealt with. Indeed, I hadn't considered it was rape at the time and it took a while for me to believe that it was. The term 'date rape' hadn't been coined back then. I blamed myself totally, as indeed some people still might today.

I was seventeen or eighteen years old, had been drunk and feeling rejected by my boyfriend who had dumped me. I had been dancing in a flirtatious way and I had accepted an invitation to go to a party in a town ten miles away with a man I had never met before. I hadn't a clue where I was geographically. I soon sobered up when I realised there was no party and that he had brought me there to go to bed with him. He was insistent, and although I said, no, I didn't want to have sex with him, he didn't listen. Because I was terrified and didn't know where I was and didn't know what else to do I didn't fight back. He was, after all, bigger than me and there was nobody else in the house to come to my rescue. He did at least take me home afterwards.

I told nobody what had happened; I just wanted to run away from the situation. So I left home and went to live with my aunty in London. My parents talked me out of joining the army, which was my first idea of escape. I found work and somewhere else to live in a house share. However, my ex-boyfriend came to visit one weekend, and never went home. We returned to our home town to get married. I loved him, but I think subconsciously I blamed him as well for the rape as there were a few rocky moments in our relationship during that time. After all, if he hadn't dumped me, I wouldn't have gone out that night etc.

I no longer blame him – he was not responsible for my actions or those of the man. But I think that because of the shame I felt and the way that I had given myself totally to my boyfriend, which is what I believe sexual intercourse is really all about, I didn't think that anyone else would have me. I didn't feel I deserved the white wedding of a pure virgin. How times and attitudes have changed! I include this part of my story to illustrate for the younger readers how ingrained some of these attitudes are in some of us who are older.

Indeed, research shows that "heterosexual vaginal intercourse is less meaningful than it used to be. Until the 1950s vaginal intercourse was generally used as an expression of lifelong commitment in marriage. The belief that you can have sex without getting pregnant developed some time after the 1960s with the introduction of the pill. By the year 2001, the average age of first intercourse was sixteen for both sexes while the average age of marriage was twenty-eight for women and thirty for men (*National Survey of Sexual Attitudes and Lifestyles 2000* and Office for National Statistics). An act of heterosexual vaginal intercourse in the context of the belief that you might make a baby takes on a different significance from the same act in the context of the belief that nothing like that could ever happen – or if it does you could always have an abortion."[6]

Our sexuality is very much part of who we are and therefore will link in with our spirituality. If we have been damaged sexually then that will have a knock-on effect spiritually. For me it took a long time to trust, to believe I was worthy of being loved and to receiving love, be that sexual or otherwise.

By the end of university in 2000 the call to ordination had returned. So I attended another selection conference; different people, different place, different outcome. They said they couldn't see anything of what the previous selectors had picked up and had no hesitation in recommending me. I believe the selector the first time round, who gave us all a hard time pressed my internal buttons on the hurt that the car accident brought to the surface because when I came out from her, and indeed on the way home, I felt I'd been violated in a similar way to that earlier trauma of being raped.

In autumn 2000 I started my training at St John's College, Nottingham. The big chip on my shoulder about being thick as two short planks wasn't quite as big (although it was still there and had to have some shaving/sanding down thanks to a few weeks of counselling).

CHAPTER 6
At Theological College

April 2001 – retreat at Loyola Hall, which started on Easter Day

We had had a quiet day in college a few weeks before this retreat. When I met with my director for the retreat, she gave me some prayers to use the first evening and day. To my surprise one was the same as one we'd had at college that had provoked difficult feelings in me. I thought now, 'Here we go again!' I knew that God was going to be at work in me in the retreat, going back into healing again those deep, deep scars.

But did I want to be healed? Better the devil you know, as they say. I'd become used to the way I was. Letting God heal me meant I'd have to be different. A challenge! I tried to use a meditation on Jesus healing the paralytic but to no avail. It didn't happen/work. During Holy Communion that evening I felt that the verses "Do not call anything impure that God has made clean" (Acts 10:15) referred to me. God has cleansed me, so I shouldn't consider myself unclean. Once again I tried the meditation and this time there was a certain amount of 'success'. In my imagination, as I enter the Bible story, I am taken into a house by friends and Jesus touches me and heals me. I don't feel any emotion, but nevertheless thank him, and write a poem titled *Resurrection* in which I state that I am NOT a victim nor a survivor. I am a woman made in God's image. I am made to be vulnerable, hurt and pained; to be healed and restored, cherished and loved. And it is Jesus' love which has done this. He has borne my grief and pain. So, with him, I can rise again in the Easter victory over death.

The next day I felt challenged to really let Jesus heal me. I eventually settled into the meditation again. This time Jesus appeared like a surgeon in a green gown and mask, although not impersonal and professional, he touched me as a doctor taking a smear sample, not a lover. I noticed a book in the room with an icon and a eucharistic prayer written in Latin. I thought about how it is through His body and blood that we receive healing – by His wounds, ours are healed. I decided to take this thought with me to the communion service.

In the gallery overlooking the chapel I asked Jesus to show me how he sees me, how he saw me developing into a woman. His reply was very long. He told me how he was with me, watching me make mistakes and develop, how he saw me fall in love with my husband and that he had given him to me as the love of my life, that I was strong enough for him, to love him and that I would see again what I loved in him, if I will let go of the hurt and pain. Jesus suggested, "Think of life's irritations and pain as the way the pearl that is you is formed. You, Liz, are a priceless pearl: my great treasure." He continued to tell me all the positives He sees in me, adding, "I know you don't agree with me on this – but one day, soon, you will be able to hear these words and accept them: *You are my beloved, my beautiful one. I love you just as you are.*"

Communion was peaceful and joyful. Indeed, the priest commented afterwards on my joyful face during singing the hymn, *Alleluia, alleluia, give thanks to the risen Lord*. I imagined that as the bread and wine went through my body it would further the healing, and I consciously let go of any hurt, regrets, bitterness or resentment which I may have still been holding onto. I imagined them flowing out of me.

Life is to be lived...

That evening I went into the art room. I felt restless, not at all artistic so started off with a scribble/doodle that I coloured in. I continued to work on it during the rest of the retreat and it was on my study wall for a few years as a reminder of not to take life too seriously – it is to be lived and fun, even when it doesn't make any sense. And right in the middle is the reminder to 'be still'. The dark purple circle at the bottom right was a 'mistake'. I'd picked up a different type of crayon: but God takes our mistakes and uses them. It turned into an image of the tomb, out of which Lazarus came – and I come – to stand in the light of God's healing.

"OK, Lord, you win – I don't look too bad."

An early morning brisk walk around the field, praising God enabled me to consider that I am wonderfully made. God, the potter, has made me as I am. Who am I to argue with him? A walk in the grounds showed me the variety of trees – God has made them all different. It would be boring if they were all the same. And the more interesting ones are those with branches that have been damaged, not the trees which are perfectly symmetrical. But we are not interested in the storms or diseases which have affected the tree, or why some branches may have been pruned because they were in the way. What we see is a how the tree is now – not what it was years before. And if there is so much beauty and interest in a tree, as it is now, the product of its history, how much more interesting is a person, who they are now.

I am the way I am now because of the way I have been formed, both nature and nurture, good and bad events and influences. God has formed me, Elizabeth Jane Fairless, he has made me in my mother's womb from the egg and sperm of my parents and he has watched me grow and guided me on my way through life. I am who I am, now, present tense and linear, ongoing. Who I am now, is not who I have been, nor who I will be, but a stage upon the way. As with all of God's creation, I am good, well made and functional. I serve a purpose, I have my uses.

But I can only see a part of me. I don't see the whole picture; I don't see me as others do because I hear those negative voices who deny that I am wonderfully made. Why do we separate things into self-exclusive categories: functional/beautiful? Very few things do not have a certain beauty, and often the beauty and interest, comes with age and use. I am such a thing – I have a beauty which arises from age and use, not the porcelain doll beauty, nor photographic model beauty, but mine is the beauty which is in the eye of the beholder. And I know that God looks on me and sees beauty, even though I don't see it. I accept that my perception of myself is not the same as others.

Although the picture of the potter is scriptural (Jeremiah 18), it is too pre-deterministic/controlling a picture of God. I prefer to think of Him as a gardener who sometimes prunes and trains a plant and sometimes leaves it to grow where it will. God didn't cause my accident but did cause the first Church Selectors to say "no". Equally devastating events and both times God helped me to bring good from them. I am thankful for both as they've brought me to where I am and who

I am today. However, we plants should not try and tell the gardener what to do, where to put us or when and how to prune. He knows how we will turn out – He knows from experience how each individual plant will develop and what are the best growing conditions – we do not.

Later that day I meditated on the woman at the well (John 4:5–42). How does Jesus see me? I imagined Jesus coming to me for water. I was unable to look him in the eyes, I felt ashamed. My second attempt showed me that I still had some way to go to fully be healed as I still had negative thoughts about myself. When I asked Jesus why I couldn't see what he could see in me, he said the reason I couldn't was because I have bandages over my eyes. So I do a meditation on the raising of Lazarus (John 11:43–44). However, at the point when I (as Lazarus) come out of the tomb and the bandages are removed, I have no eyes! How unfair! My subconscious is still resisting and I feel cross.

At the end of the evening communion service, I thought God was saying I should draw a self-portrait that night. He must be kidding! But, as I had prayed for a miracle and asked to be able to see, I supposed I must try. So I did, despite it being eight p.m. and extremely tired and my eyes hurting. Being on retreat is no holiday! Afterwards I had to admit, "OK Lord, you win – I don't look too bad."

I decided that the next day I should take things easy, have a quiet day, working on my cross-stitch sampler. In the afternoon I wander into the lounge for a quick look at the books. I'm drawn to Jim Cotter's *Healing: more or less*. I flick through and one prayer in particular touched me deep within. I shed a single tear; no more would come, even though I wasn't too concerned about what other people thought. I was tense inside; I could feel that something was happening but I didn't know what. In my head I sang, "Be still and know that I am God… who healeth thee… in thee O Lord do I put my trust". I sat and relaxed as best I could and invited God to continue with what He was doing. After all, I had prayed "take me to people, events and situations…" perhaps there was a reason for doing that there and then. I was feeling slightly confused, thinking that God had healed me two days before. I was learning that with very deep issues such as mine it can take several times of prayer for healing. It's a step at a time, or like peeling layers of an onion.

During the retreat I had a foot massage from a nun. During it I imagined it was Jesus touching my feet. She didn't actually kiss me, as it implies in the poem that I wrote, but in my imagination, Jesus was washing my feet like he did the disciples' feet in the upper room.

I conclude that because I am made in God's image, the great I AM, then that makes me a smaller I AM. Smaller, less significant than He by far, but, nevertheless, a special I AM. I have been told to be still… be BOLD… be STRONG, but was afraid. And again, be still, be loved, be served. I had managed during this retreat to be still and had heard Him affirming me and that He loves me, just as I am. So I left the retreat knowing that I am a woman, loved by God, precious in His eyes and of infinite worth. I had learnt to be still and now I heard His voice say just BE. The answer to 'who am I?' is 'I am me'.

Lent 2002

Reflecting on the journey so far and realizing that I'm now more able to rest in God's love, I recognize that His love will never let me go; He is my fortress and my strength. I trust in

Him and I give Him back the life He's given me that in the ocean depths of His love, my life will be richer and fuller. I realise that I share in the wonderful and amazing life of the Trinity by virtue of the Holy Spirit dwelling within me!

However, a couple of weeks later I was down in the depths of despair once more. I wished I were dead. I wanted everything to go away and leave me alone. No decisions. No writing. No thinking. No nothing – obliterate everything – cease to be. I felt that's what I should be: dead and gone.

CHAPTER 7
Life as a Curate Brings Stress

I was ordained as a deacon at Lichfield Cathedral on 29th June 2002 and started my life as a curate. The first year was enjoyable and went well. On 21st June 2003 I was ordained as a priest.

April 2003 – individually guided retreat at Loyola Hall

I was once more depressed, stressed and just wanting to rest. I had been upset on Mothering Sunday as I no longer had a mum and my daughters were no longer at home, and was still low on retreat. However, during a walk, whilst praying, I felt God sing to me, *I will always love you* to *The Bodyguard* tune. I picked a daffodil, imagining it was from God. I also picked one for my mum. I dried and framed them as a reminder of that moment of Grace and consider the idea that God is my mother.

During the retreat I also did a painting depicting my pain but I put it in the bin as I had taken with me the important message of new life coming from the pain – that could stay in the bin! Over the years I have kept journals where I have poured out my pain in words. As part of the process of writing this book, and of needing to move on, I burnt them, releasing the memories that went with them. I have kept the artwork and a few pages where they had been attached. One is from this retreat with part of a picture of daffodils noting that if I wish to be alive, I must learn to die at every moment, that is, to say goodbye, let go, move on.

At the Clergy Conference in April on the theme of Conflict and Reconciliation, we were blessed by The Most Reverend John Sentamu's reflection. He spoke of the need for inner stillness and security and a balance between the ego, id and superego. We need to yield to God (Romans 5). From this position we are able to withstand conflicts around us. I was aware of inner conflict, of my 'inner child' wanting attention, of wanting to be loved but at the same time me not wanting or able to receive love. My spiritual director (also at the conference) was able to spend some time with me and suggested some Bible readings to use. In her opinion I was compartmentalising love, e.g. motherly, sexual, God's love.

August 2004

As the curacy draws to an end, I consider future ministry. I did two pictures reflecting the joys and sorrows of ministry and also one with my hopes for the future.

The people and ministry have been a wonderful gift from God, but sorrow and pain were never far away. Once again in a flood of tears, in the mud: "troubles without number surround me; my sins have overtaken me and I cannot see, they are more than the hairs of my head and my heart fails within me." Ps 40:12

I wonder if this is the price of ministry. Has following Jesus wrecked our marriage?

My heart fails within me. I'm heartbroken but don't know why – is it mourning the loss of love or sadness for my husband's difficulties that have tipped me out of love with him?

"I desire to do your will, O my God; your law is within my heart." Ps 40:8

There were enormous tensions within our marriage. We almost separated during the second year of curacy, but I begged him to stay. I couldn't contemplate the marriage ending then. It was too much for me to bear.

My hope for the future parish

I drew a picture thinking about what I wanted for the future and what sort of church I want next, imagining it as a garden with various plants etc. representing what I wanted. In the centre was a matchstick couple – my husband and I – holding hands, side by side, equal height, with an equality in our relationship. My priorities were: Jesus the Son of God will be our guiding light; people with mature faith; the fire of the Holy Spirit; enthusiastic people; streams of living water flowing through the church as it is one that restores; a reliable and stable core group of church members; I've got to be able to get out to countryside. And finally, I recognised that the grass is always greener on the other side. There will still be a rocky path to tread, but with God's help we'll be OK.

A Quiet Day during Holy Week, based on the hymn, My Song is Love Unknown – *March 2005*

As I reflected on the hymn, I drew a cross with figures representing my husband and daughters, and a ring. I wrote the words: All the vain things that charm me most, I sacrifice them to His blood. Sorrow and love flow mingling down.

My marriage has been important to me, hence my struggles to keep it going and not give up for twenty-eight years. The ring in the middle of the cross is the one that I had blessed and my husband gave me when we took our vows in church in 1989. The design is symbolic: three blue stones (me, him and God); four diamonds (our family); three stands of gold twisted (the Trinity). I think about the promises made and my belief that God wants healing and restoration for us.

CHAPTER 8
A Move to New Parish and Responsibilities

In June 2005 I moved to a new parish to take up two part-time posts; one as a church minister and the other as a mental health chaplain in a psychiatric hospital working mainly with the elderly and adults with a learning disability.

Am I just going round in circles? August 2005—eight-day individually guided retreat, at St Beuno's

As I went on retreat, I wanted to have a time of rest, relaxation and connecting with God. I was open to being in His presence, to deepening my prayer life. I was NOT expecting another look at my past. However, God's timing is different from ours, and He clearly had other ideas. As I pondered Psalm 23, I realised once again that God had been with me during the dark times of my life. Though I walked through the valley of the shadow of death God had been with me and His grace is enough for me. He is protecting me from the arrows of the enemy within.

I also realised that one night out of 17,567 is an insignificant proportion of my life, but its shadow has been with me since, shaping my thoughts and actions.

God knows all about me. He is familiar with all my ways. God still loves me. God was with me. God is still with me. In the deepest depths, God is there.

On the last day of the retreat, I wrote a psalm, summing up my time there. In it I praised God with all my soul. For he had heard my cries, my tears, my sighs, my pondering the same old problems, yet again needing His help, seeking Him with all my heart. He restores my soul and I trust in Him. I had come to be glad to be me. I'm called by name, I am His – adventurous, trusting Bess, perfectionist, pious Elizabeth and faithful, loving Liz. I was even able to describe myself as a rose in full bloom, delicate and sweetly perfumed, beautifully and wonderfully made and precious in His sight. In one of my meditations Jesus had kissed me on my forehead as He held my hands. As I prepared to leave the retreat and go back to normal life, I was able to say that I trust in Him as together we go forward. When rough roads and storms I have to face, I'll conquer my fears and foes in God's grace. I will not be afraid, for He is with me and I will stay in Him. He will go with me as I witness and serve in His name gathering people to Him, seeking first the kingdom of God and His righteousness; the Lord will supply my needs.

I thanked God for taking the circumstances of my life and redeeming them into the person I had become.

August 2006 – Woodbrooke Quaker Centre

I decided to go on a different type of retreat and attended an Apple Seed Course – *The Bright Field*. The focus was on using art and craft. Although I wanted to fully engage with the retreat, to enjoy art and crafts, and not do anything too 'deep', the first session saw me in tears. I was overwhelmed by feeling no good at art and that I couldn't do anything artistic.

As I had a time of prayer, I sensed God say, "BE STILL

AND KNOW THAT I AM GOD". My response was to ask God to help me to seek His face, to live a life, giving Him honour and praise.

I continued to dwell on who God is and especially the phrase, "I am who I am", as I walked round the labyrinth and collected leaves which were turning red. As I did so, I felt God say to me:

"I AM WHO I AM. I am not a god in the box, confined by hymns and books, defined by doctrine and creed. I am all you need. But… I am more than you can imagine or hope for. I am your God who creates, heals and will restore. I am He who calls you by name and loves you so much more than any human could claim. 'I am' calls out of the burning bush – take off your shoes for you stand on holy ground."

As I approach God through Jesus, he takes off the dirty shoes of sin, purifying me within so I may stand before the throne of Grace and dare to gaze upon His face.

Clergy Advent Quiet Day – Hawkstone Hall – 7 December 2006

By December 2006 I had become very tired and depressed. I was too drained, too down on myself to change. I knew my faults, my failings, my feeble attempts at holiness. The shepherds brought lambs and the wise men brought precious gifts. All I had was inner turmoil and stress and so I lay them at His feet.

Retreat August 2007 at Noddfa, Penmaenmawr.

This was not my usual Individual Guided Retreat but a preached-journaling retreat based on the life of Ignatius Loyola led by Billy Hewett, SJ.

I meditated on Psalm 84 verse 2 "My soul yearns, even faints, for the courts of the Lord; my heart and my flesh cry out for the living God" and I realised that I am blessed because my strength is in Him. As the rain pours down, so blessings pour on me and within me as I open my heart to receive, and trust in Him.

As I looked at the stone wall in the chapel, the beauty of the stones – big and small – reminded me of all the times of my life: the big things that I remember and the small ones forgotten which have left their mark and have their place as part of me. This time at Noddfa is another stone in the mosaic of my life – a precious stone, many faceted, glimmering in the light of God's love.

As a girl I sat halfway up the stairs at Nan's. As I look back now, I can see that although I wasn't aware of it then, Jesus was with me every time I was alone and sad or crushed. My Jesus, my best friend, my big brother, I love you more than any other. Thank you for always being there for me and with me. I remember one time when I was at secondary school and ran away from home. I'd been bullied at school and rather than tell someone and get help, I ran away. I got as far as Derby bus station, and was sitting in the bus shelter. I'd run out of money and fags and was drawn to an advert for The Samaritans. I rang them up and was reunited with my parents. Years later, reflecting on this, I realised that Jesus had been there with me in the bus shelter.

An afternoon walk on the beach gives time to reflect on the retreat. It's been difficult mixing the elements of quiet personal reflection, group sharing, input from the leader – and making time to rest and relax. I wrote two poems that came to me, fairly easily and quickly as I walked on the beach. I was praising God and thankful for the Rock of my Salvation, Jesus. I know His promises hold true to be with me always, in all places, whatever my mood. How often though I stand in one place and expect God to come to me in the old familiar ways when <u>He</u> wants to do something new. As I stood still right by the edge of the sea, watching the ebb and flow I became aware of God's love being like waves and that quite often the waves of His love recede, and with each rolling one He seems further away. So I need to keep on moving forward on my pilgrimage of faith to stand in the waves of God's love. God is my rock and my fortress in whom I trust and He brought me to the retreat house named Noddfa, which means refuge, sanctuary – a safe place.

When I had arrived, I had wondered if God would be there. It had been a good time of meeting people from various places. I had spent time learning and laughing as well as listening to God my mother, Jesus my brother and the Holy Spirit, my friend. I had also shed many tears of sorrow and sadness, pain and anguish and in the calm after the storm, experienced peace, stillness and healing Grace.

The tide was going out and my retreat was coming to an end and – just when I think I have the measure of God I'm surprised by a wave of His love, unexpected, it reached me, lapping at my feet. Not engulfing but caressing me, teasing out the woman He's made me to be. Without any doubt, I had met God on this retreat.

As I looked at the beach with various-sized rocks and stones on the sand I considered that they were formed by the action of the sea slowly changing them. I remembered the shining crystal chandelier in the lounge at the retreat house, and that sand is used to make glass. In a similar way, God takes us and smoothes down the rough edges. As His love ebbs and flows in our lives, healing our memories, we are also transformed into fine crystals that can sparkle with God's love.

May 2008 – Reflecting upon my childhood

I had thought about writing this book for a long time. I almost started in 2008 and in preparation, at the suggestion of my spiritual director, spent some time reflecting upon my childhood.

Mum, Dad, Andy and me – a suburban family with a dog called Penny who I loved. The memories are there – lying deep within – perhaps I should let sleeping dogs lie lest they jump up and bite if I poke and prod. But I'm curious. I want to know what lies deep within, what happened to shape me into the person I am today.

I am who I am because of who I've been. I've been hurt; I've been smacked, but not too much; enough for discipline, enough to know what it's like but not so much as to be permanently damaged. All the knocks, setbacks and hang-ups are all part of the human condition. And I've been loved, worried over, protected and raised by parents who wanted me, loved me, and cared for me. They did their best, were 'good enough' parents.

And that's all anyone can ask. I thank God for my Mum and Dad. I lived a normal ordinary humdrum life: happy days and sad, playing outside, running free through fields and woods till it's time for tea. Friends came and went: my first best friend Pearl at infant school and Christopher at the bottom of the street. Then the move to the Midlands, wanting to fit in and be liked, accepted. Donna and Douglas, Gail and Anne. Fallings out and making up, teenage years were not much fun.

Holidays by the sea and days out with Nan and Granddad – "Are we there yet?" "You'll wish your life away" en route to Brighton with its pebbly beach. Years later I learn the poem *I must go down to the sea again, to the lonely sea and the sky…* – I still love to be by the sea and feel its calming influence.

I was a chubby child – with dirty knees – living at No 8 Stanton Close. Happy days playing in the street with Christopher whose garden had huge sunflowers. But then one day running away from home, splashing in puddles and being startled by a frog, I was sent running back – into the safety of home.

I look at the photos and feel sad. A small child with a very bad haircut stares back at me, looking glum. There's no sparkle, no sense of fun or enjoyment of the moment, no captured joy like there is in photos of my daughters. I know it's me, but I feel detached. My childhood is like a darkened room in which there's a flickering light so that odd glimpses of the past are illuminated. Perhaps I should leave it at that.

Retreat July 2008 – Nether Springs, Northumbrian Community

I arrived at the retreat house feeling very tired from working hard and just wanted to rest and pray, as reflected in my first painting. I had been using the Celtic Daily Prayer of the community and thought it would be good to visit them. However, it turned out to be an emotional time.

I did another painting. The first stage was a chaotic mess of colours which reflected my emotions. Confronted with the depths of pain within me I ran out of the grounds, down the lane and kept on running until I could run no more. Later on, after prayer and realising there was hope, I added to it words about new life.

Towards the end of the retreat a poem from their monthly cycle of meditations spoke to me: Arise, my love, my fair one. Song of Songs 2:10. Jesus was once again inviting me to accept His love. But I was unable to receive love.

The young lady who led my retreat suggested that her mother, who lived near to me, might be able to help me further. She had many years of experience of praying for people and a ministry of deliverance. I saw her three times, each one of benefit in getting to the root of my inability to receive love. She prayed for me to be delivered/ healed from a curse on the family. This was a surprise, as you can imagine. My task since then has to be practice loving myself (not easy).

CHAPTER 9
2009: The Year My Life Radically Changed

My dad died very suddenly and unexpectedly in January 2009. He had been a fit and healthy eighty-year-old who still did athletics and within twenty-four hours, died. The family was in a state of shock. I got through the funeral and grieving as best I could and was helped to come to terms with the loss by times of prayer and Bible reading. One of the surprising things was realising that I was an orphan.

I was drawn to verses 10-11 in Psalm 45: "Listen, daughter, and pay careful attention: Forget your people and your father's house. Let the king be enthralled by your beauty; honour him, for he is your lord."

I was reminded that I'm a daughter of the Most High–adopted, a full heir, born of the spirit, not of human decision. God himself is my Father. Although no longer, humanly speaking, a daughter (a thought which is painful), I am God's daughter, His beloved in whom He is well pleased. Years ago, He showed me this truth when meditating on a church window showing Jesus' baptism and applied those words to me. Ties to my childhood home were still strong, despite when I'd worked through issues before ordination, thinking I'd cut them.

July 2009 – holiday and returning to work

After three weeks' holiday, during which I'd scattered Dad's ashes in the first week, and received a cheque for my inheritance at the end of the last one, I found returning to work very difficult. After two weeks I admitted I needed help and went to my GP who prescribed antidepressants and four weeks off work.

I felt a failure, that I'd squandered my spiritual inheritance by not attending to prayer and working in my own strength and not God's. My relationship with God had dwindled, I thought. As my mood lifted, I could see how bad I'd become. During a prayer time considering the parable of the prodigal son (Luke 15:11–31) I felt I was in the pig sty, realising the need to go home but fearful of the reception I'd receive. Would I be welcomed, or would I be treated like the servant in the parable of the talents (Matthew 25:14–30) and be thrown out to the wailing and gnashing of teeth? Walking with my dog in a field and picking a buttercup I realised that God's attitude to me is… "consider the lilies… don't worry… Your heavenly father knows what you need."

God also spoke through Isaiah 30:15–18: "In repentance and rest is your salvation, in quietness and trust is your strength, but you would have none of it…" I realised that I had let prayer slip. I had been busy with my agenda, my plans and 'stuff' perhaps more than God's. "Yet the Lord longs to be gracious to you therefore He will rise up to show you compassion. For the Lord is a God of justice. Blessed are all who wait for Him."

I decide not to return to work until after a retreat that I had booked. I wasn't sure whether to go or not. My GP agreed it would be good for me. She was right. I was to discover that

God was certainly 'on my case'.

My director is an Anglican priest – therefore he will understand my situation better than a lay person or a Catholic priest. To my amazement that wasn't all. He had previously had ten years' experience as a mental health chaplain and before being ordained was a psychiatric nurse. I relaxed. I was clearly in safe hands, with a man who would not only understand my two workplaces, but have the necessary skills to handle my depressed and stressed state of mind. My only dilemma was, should I admit to him my suicidal thoughts? Would he have me 'sectioned'? (The Mental Health Act allows someone to be admitted, detained and treated in hospital against their wishes.) The last thing I wanted was to end up at Shelton as a patient. He assured me that he was no longer licensed and therefore couldn't. What a relief!

Every day, almost without fail, the reading he set me and the focus he suggested was also backed up or reflected some way by either my daily lectionary readings (a published list for church use) which I always looked at after doing the reflection he'd suggested or by something in the afternoon worship. It might be the reading, something the preacher said or a hymn. It was amazing. So many 'coincidences' add up to God's guidance.

I expressed my thoughts in collage and drawing rather than poetry. I felt broken, like a branch of the vine almost broken off. Whilst walking one day I noticed how beautiful a broken tree trunk looked with its branches and twigs covered in moss shining in the sun. So I collected some of the twigs to remind me of how even broken things can be beautiful. I arranged them on a piece of paper and wrote: Beauty in Brokenness.

One day I was reminded of a hymn based on words of scripture: "Lift up your heads you gates that the King of glory may come in" which triggered off other hymns and words of scripture. The result is the picture King of Glory upon which the following is written:

WHO IS THE KING OF GLORY? JESUS CHRIST – The Servant King. The earth is the Lord's and everything in it. He made himself nothing. He washed their feet, became human, obedient to death. At the name of Jesus every knee shall bow. JESUS CHRIST IS LORD and I invited Him in. And he invited me…

Towards the end of the retreat, I went to receive God's peace through the sacrament of reconciliation. I was not so much weighed down with a sense of guilt, but wanted to 'off-load' negative thoughts and resentments and hurts of the recent months. I wasn't given a penance to do. I expect my retreat director felt he'd given me sufficient. However, I felt the need to do something. I'd still got the list of 'sins' in my back pocket and had no desire to go around with them. The image of being a broken branch of the vine needing to be thrown on the fire was still with me. I wanted to burn the sins in some way to symbolise their forgiveness. As this wasn't practical, I buried the paper under a holly and ivy bush in the woods near the house and then called to mind the poem *Love bade me welcome* (by George Herbert). I'd been given it as a penance some years previously by my spiritual director. By 'coincidence' a priest said something to me as I entered the house. This was unusual as it was on the silent corridor. So I asked him where I might find the poem and he directed me to a library I wasn't aware of. I soon found the poem and used it whilst looking at the icon of the Trinity, imagining sitting and eating with God.

As I read the introduction to the poet's book on the rule of holy life and character of a priest, I had one of those 'wow' moments. His book paints a picture of a priest who is perfect in every way: a clerical Mary Poppins who displays all the virtues of Christ. That sort of thing is not good for a priest who is depressed as we all know we are far from perfect and don't need to be reminded of our shortcomings. However, he explains why:

"... our saviour hath made the argument of a pastor's love... the character of a true pastor, that I may have a mark to aim at: which also I will set as high as I can, since he shoots higher that threatens the moon than he that aims at a tree. Not that I think, if a man do not all which is here expressed, he presently sins and displeases God, but that it is a good strife to go as far as we can in pleasing of him who hath done so much for us."

Reading this made me realise that it isn't a sin to not be perfect. That realisation took a weight off me and had a healing effect.

2nd September – I consider returning to work.

Whilst walking my dog I picked up a pheasant's feather. It reminded me of the uplifting words in Isaiah 40. "Those who hope in the LORD will renew their strength. They will soar on wings like eagles; they will run and not grow weary, they will walk and not be faint." (verse 31)

However, I felt more like a pheasant or game bird that's hiding in the long grass, fearful that if I started to fly I'd be shot down. One of the images I'd had on retreat was that of being a bird with a broken wing, unable to fly. This was added to when after a night of very little sleep – possibly the worst I had there – I opened my Bible to pray using the lectionary for that day only to burst out laughing as I read from Psalm 102 verse 7 – "I lie awake; I have become like a bird alone on a roof."

For many years I have found comfort in the image of God sheltering me under His wing. With these thoughts in mind, I created a collage using feathers with these words:

I lay awake like a bird alone on a roof unable to fly with a broken wing. I hoped in God. In the shelter of His wings my heart began to sing. I caught a glimpse of what will be – one day I'll soar on the wind of the Holy Spirit like an eagle.

October 2009 – a shocking diagnosis (yet one making sense)

In October 2009 my GP diagnosed that the root of my stress and depression was not the combination of grief and trying to do two stressful jobs, it was my marriage. She sat back at her desk, put her hands together (almost as if in prayer) looked me in the eye and said, "You're not going to like this. You've got to stop papering over the cracks of your marriage". The image that came to my mind was that it wasn't cracks but gaping holes. It was as if we'd had a hole in the floorboards covered with a rug and each time we walked over it, it dipped down and now I'd fallen right through.

I had already had one session of counselling to try and get to the roots of my reactions to memories of being bullied. On the second session I suggested we look at my ending the marriage.

November 2009

Upon considering whether or not to go to a memorial service (All Souls) at the church where Dad's name would be read out, I weigh up the merits of going or not. As I considered the area where I grew up and the bungalow we lived in, I realised that there was nobody there. In a dream I saw empty streets, well-kept lawns and front gardens. The people living there are new. Although I have in-laws and old friends in the town, they are not my flesh and blood; no one of my family line is there. So I conclude that I can light a candle and say a prayer at home. I also battled to overcome negative thoughts and the need for perfectionism that had arisen that weekend.

After much soul searching and with the help of the counsellor over several weeks, prayer and consulting with trusted friends, I reached the decision to end the marriage. What I took to be confirmation of this came during a bath and meditating on Jesus calming the storm (Mark 4:35–41). Although I felt the time was right, my husband didn't agree so I stormed out of the house and went to stay with a friend. When I returned the next morning (5 November 2009) he had gone.

Phoning the bishop to inform him was not the most comfortable of conversations. However, the level of support received from Lichfield Diocese was wonderful. I couldn't have asked for more. I had time off work to reflect and recover. I was not in a fit state to be ministering to others.

CHAPTER 10
The Start of a New Phase of Life as Separated

It was Advent, the start of a new church year and the start of my new life without my husband. It got off to a good start with the traditional Advent service at a cathedral with my cousin and her daughter on my way to the Sheldon Community (Society of Martha and Mary) for a two-week stay. The focus for me was twofold: looking to the future, praying that God will guide me; and reflecting on the past to see where God has been active and where I needed to repent and seek forgiveness and healing.

I felt as if I was in the wilderness, tired and in need of rest. I was in comfortable rooms named Mary's Lodge. I think it appropriate that just as Mary sat at Jesus' feet, so I too need to sit and be still in His presence rather than rushing around being a busy Martha. I sing the Advent hymn, *O come, O come Emmanuel and ransom captive Israel.*

How I felt when I arrived to reflect on the breakdown of my marriage resulted in a picture of blackness and pain.

I cry out to God, feeling especially low the first week. Sarah, the person accompanying me with a couple of hours of one-to-one time over the fortnight, prescribes Pleasure as the focus. Learning to rest, relax and enjoy myself doesn't come easily or naturally. By Friday of the first week, I have to admit to having slipped from grief and tiredness into depression. Pleasure escapes me – no pain, no pleasure, no anger, no sadness – stuck in neutral going nowhere. After watching a bit of a film about young love I had to switch it off – painful reminders of being fifteen and falling in love with my husband. Saturday, listening to the radio a song prompts me to feel very sad that I'm hurting him so much. Tears flow and I'm not really sure why, or what I'm feeling.

A line from a film strikes me – "all life is, is four or five days that change everything." At first, I agree, then as I think it through, I decide that it isn't the days that change everything, but how we let them, how we react and let them inform and direct us. I list the important days for me:

1. giving myself to my boyfriend (who I later married)
2. having him back when he dumped me
3. being raped by a stranger
4. not telling my boyfriend to go when he visited me in London (a weekend visit turned into him moving in)
5. getting married
6. saying Yes to Jesus

And now I've got a seventh day to add: when I told my husband it was over, and meant it.

I drew a timeline and graph of important dates from the age of fifteen to then, add times of professional counselling and when prescribed antidepressants. The graph shows highs and lows of the marriage. The longest periods without any important dates, is three years 1986–7–8 (but in that time I gave my life to Jesus which is the most important, positive, but I can't give an exact date) and 2006–7–8. The graph has got far more lows than highs and only one period since the wedding and pre-children days of marriage when I put the positives above a base line of neutral. But there would have been times, on odd days, when they would have gone over. I did it quickly – a gut reaction rather than detailed analysis of diary entries, so probably more an indicator of how I feel while drawing the graph than what I felt over the years.

On the Sunday I went to Exeter Cathedral for Holy Communion. It was good to get up early and be out. I cried at the confession because of the pain I was causing my husband and also during the eucharistic prayer at the reminder that I was unable to preside. I purposely sat as close to the altar as I could (we were in the choir stalls and seating up by the high altar).

Monday brought a turning point. I felt more positive, thanks to the time with Sarah on Sunday afternoon. During a walk in the rain, I observed the water running down a path to a gate, turning the path into a stream. In time would it become a river? I wondered about well-worn paths and the erosion of familiar ways. Over time they change into ways that are no longer safe to walk; so we have to change our route. Behaviour has to change eventually. The well-worn familiar habits of our marriage had become 'un-walk-able'.

During my prayer time on Tuesday, which I went to with a completely open mind, no pre-set notions or emotions to bring to God, I take off my wedding ring and place it on the altar asking God to release me from the vows I'd taken. This was prompted by Psalm 56:12 "I will fulfil my vows to you, O God" I realised once more that I hadn't fulfilled the marriage vows, and I sang, *Please release me, let me go, for I don't love you anymore. To live a lie would be a sin, release me, and let me love again.*

When I'd stopped crying, I turned to the Old Testament

and Isaiah 30. I read it with my situation in mind and the thought that our marriage had become an idol, represented by the gold wedding ring. The perfect wife, the ideal marriage doesn't exist, we all know this. But, somehow, I had clung on; obedient to the vows, those promises – but what I was doing was staying married but NOT actually fulfilling the vows. Remaining married had become the goal, not the result of the relationship. I'm reminded of the picture I did when meditating on *When I Survey the Wondrous Cross*. My marriage was one of the "vain things that charm me most."

As I read from Isaiah 30 I felt the words of verses 19–22, were aimed at me: Liz "… you will weep no more. How gracious he will be when you cry for help! As soon as he hears, he will answer you" verse 19. "Although the Lord gives you the bread of adversity and the water of affliction [*this marriage]*…" verse 20. "Whether you turn to the right or to the left, your ears will hear a voice behind you, saying, 'This is the way; walk in it.'" Verse 21. "Then you will desecrate your idols… your images covered with gold [*wedding ring, marriage*]; you will throw them away like a menstrual cloth and say to them, 'Away with you!'" verse 22.

I wonder: Is this confirmation that I'm doing the right thing, or a coincidence? At the end of my prayer time, I wrap the rings in a tissue – and put them in one of the sanitary waste bags back in the lodge. I didn't throw them away literally, but have put them in a safe place.

I slept the whole night through without waking up! I felt positive and made a plan for the day. I felt at peace and had a good day.

The next day, however, I woke early with a headache. I consider broken vows and the subject of idols again. I looked back through my journal to Easter 2004 when my husband and I almost split up. He was going to leave me but I begged him to stay. Why did I do that having prayed for years that he would leave me? The only answer to my question was that perhaps I had lacked security in myself and relationship with God. I had clung on to the marriage idol, feared the future without my husband, needed to feel loved and feared being left and abandoned (a childhood fear). So he didn't leave and I felt peaceful and happy. However, only two weeks later I was wishing myself dead.

The words of the preacher on Good Friday 2004 had struck me. Broken promises (as in wedding vows) are as if broken to Jesus, who said, *whatever you do to the least of these you do to me* (Matthew 25:40–45). The marriage vows are to love, honour, cherish, obey. I considered the marriage vows and concluded that they do not mean we should remain married for the sake of remaining married.

Jesus' teaching on divorce is very brief (Matthew 5). It seems that a man can only divorce his wife if there's been sexual immorality. He doesn't actually say adultery. Biblical scholars will know the Greek better than me, but this is how I understood it at the time.

Our marriage's sexual relationship had been damaged. I took into the marriage the results of another man's immorality. And my husband took his 'baggage'. I gave myself to him sexually, 100% for love, imagining commitment for life and he dumped me and went with another girl (I presumed they had sex). Does all that count as sexual immorality? If so, I feel that's my legalistic 'get out' clause. But, does that still count if I forgave him and we made our vows in church in 1989? More questions than answers! So I turn to God and feel him speak through words of scripture and a picture of a heart containing some hands and a butterfly. "Behold, God is my helper; it is the Lord who upholds my life... An offering of a free heart will I give you and praise your name, O Lord, for it is gracious." (Psalm 54:4 and 7)

I was also reminded of Isaiah 61 where God promises a crown of beauty, the oil of joy and a garment of praise, and drew myself wearing a gold dress with my hands raised in praise and worship.

I never got my happy ever after. Try as I did, and I did try to love him, it just hasn't happened. I felt very sad. However, with Jesus there is New Life, Hope for the future – Resurrection! During a meditation of the raising of Lazarus I imagined myself coming out of the tomb, as Lazarus. I also prayed: "The Lord be gracious to me. I long for you. Be my strength every morning."

By the end of my time at Sheldon I felt peaceful and forgiven and wrote: "God is inviting me to draw ever closer. The marriage is a branch no longer producing good fruit, so it is to be cut off and burnt. I am responding once more to the call of Jesus as the lover in Song of Songs, to Him knocking at the door of my heart, inviting me to sit and taste His meat. I don't know what the future holds, but I do know that Jesus is still calling me, drawing me from within on cords of love."

January to April 2010 was spent in quiet prayer, resting and working through the pain of separation. I had some professional counselling sessions to help with the grief and one of the exercises was to perform a 'funeral' for the marriage. I wrote some prayers and a letter which I burnt, burying the ashes in the compost heap with the words of committal "earth to earth, ashes to ashes etc." I committed to God all the regrets and things to be forgiven in the sure knowledge that His love does indeed cover a multitude of sins. There was still sadness but also peace.

I spent time in walking with God, trying to discern the future of ministry and what He had in store for me. The book *Healing the Purpose of Your Life* by Linn was helpful in this. I am a priest with 'sealed orders' to bring people into a deeper relationship with God. I am a fulfillment of Isaiah 61.

I returned to work on 10 February 2010. It was a gradual return, with a renewed sense of God's calling and purpose for my life. A couple of days before this I had spent time praying and meditating in the Ignatian way of imagining myself in a Bible story with Jesus. He was walking through the crowds, healing people. It was difficult for me to fully picture but I 'felt' Him approach me and I was unsure if He would stop, but He did. I was with my spiritual director and a close friend. Jesus took my face in His hands, kissed my head, told me He was healing me and that it was a slow process. He will never leave me. He is with me in my friends. I should build relationships, enjoy life, play (I could hear children playing in the school yard next door). The work will come to me in His time. I mustn't worry but be still and know that He is God, the God who *is* healing me. I felt peaceful, and as I came out of it, it was quiet; break was over and the children inside. I had been using some of my poems in my prayer times, one per day and the one for that day was *A Walk in the Park*. I made changes so it was more positive. I do appreciate myself more – I am getting better. Praise the Lord!

On the morning of my return to work I attended Holy Communion, led by the vicar. The set reading was Jesus calming the storm and telling His disciples not to be afraid. I was not afraid because I knew that Jesus was with me. Was it a coincidence that this passage is in the lectionary and set for the week I return? It was the same one that assured me the time was right to tell my husband the marriage was finally over. On that occasion I had been meditating in the bath on the calming of the storm. In my imagination I was in a yellow submarine (yes, as per the Beatles' song). Then I had pictured my husband being rescued by helicopter away from the submarine. Now, some three months later I feel that I'm back on the surface in a sailing boat with Jesus. Like a blind woman, I'm dependent on him to steer and guide me.

When Easter came, I was tired and wondering if ordained ministry had cost me my marriage – the high cost of discipleship. On the eve of Easter, I came to the end of the cycle of poems, which felt appropriate and considered the years from 1988 to 2009. They were twenty-one years of struggle and pain; of hope and joy: the journey of a lifetime, a pilgrimage of hope. It was as though I had taken the key of the door, opened it and walked through and was free. Free to discover a new me, walking hand in hand with Jesus into the future. Free to live in the resurrection.

On Easter Day my meditation took me in my imagination to a locked house. I looked out of the window and wanted to be free, so I unbolted the door – but it needed a key. I frantically looked through various rooms; they were lifeless with only furniture in. My husband was in one, watching TV so I made some tea and sat a while with him, starting to get comfy, but then got up, went through some rooms and to the front door, unlocked it and went out, running through the street. It was the road I'd grown up in. I said goodbye to my childhood house, Mum, Dad and then through the estate, to the house I'd lived in and back to the street where our first home as a married couple was. Then I was airborne and changed into a swan and eventually landed on a pond: alone. Swans mate for life. So I consider that I may be alone for the rest of my life. But I am OK with that, although a bit sad. I know that Jesus is with me. I am more fully living the resurrection life. "Lazarus" has shaken off all the grave clothes – well almost all, there was just a bit left round the ankles!

After Easter I worked through a lot of grief as I mourned the death of my marriage. However, I didn't seem depressed. There is a big difference between grief, sadness and depression. As I went through this period of bereavement there were times of feeling very low, but nevertheless trusting in God. I used meditation, being still in God's presence, to help me through it. I recognised the need to be kind to myself and after years of being told to be kind to myself I was at last managing it. I was gentle and patient with myself and letting God love me.

One of my hobbies is playing the clarinet and at the time I played in an orchestra. Whilst we went on a short holiday after Easter, I had space and time to relax but also to realise that I was still not very good at handling confrontation and that, if I had been better, then perhaps I wouldn't have put up with a dysfunctional marriage for so long. Nevertheless, I also realised how many opportunities now lay open to me for hobbies and holidays, that I hardly knew where to start! All I had wanted was to grow old with my husband and live happily ever after. But that wasn't going to happen. Life, though, is an adventure waiting for me to join in. New friends, and old, are waiting. I felt scared, as if waiting at an open door – no, I'd gone through the door. Shall I close it behind me and venture forth? Yes, I did.

Later that month, I found a clergy quiet day, led by Bishop Mark, about Grace and Frailty, helpful and well timed. The stories of Elijah (1 Kings 19) and Elisha (2 Kings) helped me to reflect on my marriage breakdown. The Bible has symbolic themes of mountain, plain and cave. The mountain tops are the great spiritual experiences, which don't happen very often so we value them when we get them, but we should not expect to spend our lives up there. We come down to the plain, the ordinariness of most of life, the everyday stuff. Then there is the cave, the place of darkness and defeat or of recovery. However, it is too easy to stay in the back of the cave. We need the challenge that sometimes comes from others who ask, "What are you doing there?" Considering what I was doing at that time, I was able to acknowledge guilt at the failure and angry questions of God. Had he really chosen my husband for me so that I could pour myself out, wear myself out and be worn down with stress and depression being married to, not the wrong man, but a lovely man, a loving demanding man who was still in many ways a child, in a dysfunctional marriage? I had so many questions and wondered where the still small voice of God was with the answers.

The Elijah story gives insight into burn out. Jezabel was the strong one in their marriage and yet she got the blame down the centuries. I was the strong one in our marriage. There tends to be great vulnerability following times of great triumph, especially in men. Life has a rhythm of rest, refreshment, rest, refreshment… we need to allow 'the angel' to minister to us. We need to allow people to help us and I am glad that over the years I have turned to others for help.

Then, considering the Elisha story – the new boy – I was

helped to consider how I face up to failure and separation, to not cling onto the past, accept what is now and trust God to steer the way forward.

I felt that I was coming up out of the depths but was very tired.

I have a tendency to work hard and put myself under pressure to achieve. I question why I can't just enjoy life. Why do I put off doing all the things for me and all the domestic stuff? There's more to life than work. I already had too many plates spinning, but was considering adding more in the form of study/research (this book). Do I try to do too much so that I set myself up for failure? So I can get stressed and depressed; to have a reason to put myself down? I concluded that I didn't deserve an easy life nor happiness because I'd done such a horrible thing to my husband. This downward spiral included not sleeping very well. However, I also held onto the need to be gentle and patient with myself and to let God heal me in His time.

In June I met my husband and he said he forgave me for hurting him and that I did the right thing for both of us in ending the marriage. I couldn't continue being the crutch for our marriage. Forgiveness is so important and I needed to hear that he forgave me. This was an important step on the way for me as I have always been very good at guilt!

By July I was again off sick. The stress of doing two jobs was too much for me and I was exhausted. I have learnt that for me depression is caused by stress. Despite that I was hopeful.

During my regular walk with the dog, I spotted new growth in an old tree stump. It gave me hope that I too would experience new growth – indeed it confirmed that I am experiencing new growth. I was like the tree – cut down but not dead.

Little did I know that during this time God was preparing me for some major healing. The preparation took the form of a dream and then being ministered to during a time of worship at a renewal conference. I had a dream where I was in an old house with crumbling metal railings on a landing and stairs. There was a toilet bowl, broken and leaking crap and toilet paper. I understood this to be the mansion that's my soul. In the dream I open a book, randomly at a page upon which is written: "If you are bereaved, come to me, my beloved bride". I couldn't read the rest and then I woke up.

When we have a dream that could be God speaking to us it is important to take it to God in prayer to seek an interpretation. So I did this, having first thought that it means God has some major renovation work to do on my soul. As part of my prayer time, I turned to the poem for the day (I had been using my poems, one per day, in turn). This day's was "I am not a victim… I'm a woman… to be healed…" Was this another coincidence? Despite continuing to pray about it I didn't get any answer. Sometimes God is frustratingly quiet.

However, during my morning walk, I reflected that I am like a puppet whose strings are being cut and I'm learning to stand on my own. The Holy Spirit will energise and guide, but I'll have free will and not be so reactive to other people's pulling on my strings.

Five days later at a renewal conference I went forward for prayer ministry. The person praying for me had a picture of a bride and God saying that he sees me as beautiful, but there is barbed wire wrapped around me. I suggest that the wire is round my heart and I feel some pressure on my chest. I feel there is a blockage stopping the cleansing flow of the Holy Spirit, and of knowing I'm loved moving from head to heart. God is giving me a crown of beauty. Two other people had words for me, to the effect that God loves me, His beloved daughter. He's pleased with me and what I've done and He's going to do more in and through me. I felt unworthy to accept a lovely white gown. So we prayed that God would show me in my next retreat what the blockage is.

As I prepared for the retreat, which was a Praying Through Film one, something I'd never done before, I felt Jesus was saying "Come away with me. Leave your books and agenda behind. Just come and rest in me. Be still. Think of the retreat as a holiday with Jesus. Chill out with me, chew the fat, watch the films. Rest. Relax. Enjoy your time alone with me, just like you've enjoyed just simply being with your girls. Go with the flow each day. No plans."

I had used my daily prayer which included Jesus saying that the Kingdom of God is like a little seed that grows, we don't know how (Mark 4:26–29). I felt God say that my healing will come in His time. I'm not to try and force it or rush it, but to rest in the soil, sunshine and watering/feeding of the Holy Spirit.

So I set off for the retreat thinking I would have a lovely rest, feeling peaceful… little did I know… looking back, I should feel that I was lulled into a false sense of security. But perhaps, God needed me to be in a relaxed and unexpectant frame of mind so that he could do what needed to be done.

Praying Through Film Retreat – July 2010

I went on this retreat with the aim of resting, relaxing and NOT doing any deep inner work. As usual, I start my retreat by walking and praying through the labyrinth, letting go and settling in. I wanted to rest and go with the flow, not strive. I hoped that I would manage it. In the labyrinth I looked ahead to see if I was nearly at the end. Jesus pointed out that I often do this instead of simply enjoying the present moment.

I didn't set out to rake over the past. Honest! God had other ideas. We watched a different film each morning, had free time the rest of the day and a time of worship and group sharing in the evening. Each day I seemed to be faced with an emotional issue.

Tuesday: *Julie & Julia.*[8] The film is about marriage, cooking, food, belief in a project and the web of relationships. I decide that I will write my book. I need to believe in myself. I can do it. I also make peace with my fifteen-year-old self and release her into God's judgment, not mine. I don't condemn her and I won't throw stones. I had been reminded of my self-criticism of embarking on sexual relationship at such a young age. God has taken my life, the little that I have to offer and is transforming it. I write the first part of a three-part poem, entitled: *A thankful heart opened a chink and let LOVE in...*

Wednesday: *Crouching Tiger, Hidden Dragon.*[9] This film has themes of kill or be killed, freedom and breaking taboos. I wonder who I am and if I am worth fighting for. I consider that I should fight the good fight. I am a warrior princess, and like Alice facing the jabberwocky. She believed six impossible things before breakfast – which six things do I believe? The dragon I have to slay is fear of love. Only I can do it. I need to find it in its lair. I need to find the superhero in me. I conclude that in quietness and rest is my strength.

Thursday: *Man on a Wire.*[10] Our marriage, as it had been for twenty-five years, underwent an enormous change when I was ordained. Too much for it to bear; it broke. It was like the wire between the towers that fell down and they had to pull it up; except we didn't manage to retrieve the marriage. I've changed. There's no going back. I have to be true to myself and I am a priest, called by God. What I do as a priest is awesome, beautiful, a gift to the church. But being a priest isn't all there is to me. Who is Liz? An adopted daughter of God, his princess, his beautiful girl. I cried for my husband and his pain. I had a 'conversation' with my inner child – she is hiding, afraid to come out and doesn't want to be forced to reconcile with him, doesn't want him back. I felt compassion for her. I prayed and felt Jesus repeating a quotation I'd heard "Beyond the ideas of right doing and wrong doing, there is a field. Come and join me there" I did two paintings: one of two fields separated by a fence, but no gate and another of me pinned under a big weight.

During the night I am awake and have the song *Totally Devoted to You* going through my mind. I change the words to fit my situation and sang it to my husband about the love he'd taken from me, my despair and wanting to die, no love to give. I used to be totally devoted him, but am no more. This became the second part of the three-part poem entitled *A Song in the Night*.

I also consider doing the two jobs. It feels like a tightrope act and events have pushed me off balance. It may seem impossible to many, but I know I can do it, with the right support and conditions, including my inner state. However, right now I feel as if I'm drowning in mud, up to my neck in it. I am crying for Help (Beatles song) I'm opening up the door... and the Holy Spirit enters.

Friday: *The Water Horse.*[11] The film has a great escape in it when the water horse, Crusoe, jumps the fence. It enables me to believe that I can too. I sing "Please release me, let me go…" Perspective is important. Where I am going, my husband isn't able to follow. He was very supportive of me following God's call to be ordained, for which I am grateful. He allowed me to grow as a person. Sitting outside, looking over the fields I see a fence and I think about the idea of befriending the thing that's feared. I have a time of silent prayer with just the mantra "be still, you're safe" which then became simply "be still". I wrote the third part of the three-part poem entitled, *Making friends with Bess.* Bess is my inner child.

I was coming to terms with the end of the marriage and I decided that instead of slaying the dragon 'fear' I would tame it, and become its friend. Riding on its back is much more adventurous than slaying it and staying where I am.

Saturday: *Philadelphia.*[12] Watching this film evoked an acknowledgement that I was fearful of male sexuality, either gay or straight. I learn that art and creativity are an aspect of sexuality. One of the other people on the retreat had a word from Jesus for me:

"Place me like a seal over your heart, like a seal on your arm; for love is as strong as death, its jealousy unyielding as the grave. It burns like blazing fire, like a mighty flame. Many waters cannot quench love; rivers cannot sweep it away." Song of Songs 8:6–7

We don't live in a courtroom – life is complex, with no simple right or wrongs most of the time. I reflected on the love I'd had from my parents and that whatever a baby grows up to do, a father will still love her. However, I felt I couldn't tell my parents that I'd been raped. They'd be disappointed, I'd let them down, and I thought God felt the same. I was dirty, spoiled and violated.

Later on, I felt uplifted when I read the whole of Song of Songs and was especially struck by the words: "do not arouse or awaken love until it so desires" that appeared several times. I am in control of my body. I also reflected that I am worthy of God's love, I have nothing to be ashamed of, that I am beautiful and precious: my vineyard is mine and I will control who enters it.

Whilst showering to prepare for Mass, I sing, *I'm gonna wash that man right out of my hair and send him on his way* (from the film *South Pacific*) and imagined washing both my husband and the man who raped me, as well as shame, away – cleansed by the Holy Spirit. I prepare for Mass as the Bride of Christ. I believe that God loves me. I receive God's love. And even if feelings tell me otherwise, I will send the enemy's lies away.

At Mass I felt that God was saying that He couldn't do everything, and that I have to receive. While someone played the cello I imagined dancing, twirling round, graceful and happy. I am Daddy's girl whom he loves. He is proud of me and all I've done. He's never been disappointed in me, always loved me, always will. I accept this as God's love and opinion too. Dad's never thought of me as second best. I cry, missing Dad, loving him and receiving his love. I feel grief without bitterness. (In 2019 I was delighted when my cousin told me that when they were at my ordination as a priest my dad had said to her how proud he was of me. As I type this it brings a tear to my eye.)

At the group sharing, I wasn't able to share the events of the day although they were uplifting and positive. I felt battered and bruised, taking responsibility for someone else in the group being upset when it was nothing to do with me. However, I was glad that happened as it revealed how I react to conflict around me. I'm reminded of the Buddhist saying: "Lotus flowers grow in muddy water. From the wounds of our hearts a beautiful flower of peace and compassion grows." I felt on trial and needed to hear and accept the group's Not Guilty verdict.

Sunday: *The Postman*.[13] When I've told my story to people, they say I am inspirational. This is an uncomfortable feeling. One of the group points out that if poems are explained they become banal. A poem needs to be able to speak to the reader so they can make their own response. So if I share my poems I need to be able to let go and for them to be interpreted, rejected or accepted. I became aware that my self-esteem was very low, and sinking. I was looking to the group to build it up, but only I can make myself feel good about myself. I also wonder if I put myself into positions where I could be rejected or criticised.

When another member of the group and I had a conflict of opinion I stormed off, but later rejoined the group when my anger subsided. When I calmed down, I realised that my self-esteem does not rely on what anyone in the group thinks of me. I didn't care what the other woman thought of me, I was protecting myself – wow – that's great, a step forward... I matter...**I** think I am worth protecting! After spending a few minutes in the chapel, quietly singing "to be in your presence, not rushing around..." I am thankful for everyone in the group. It has been a safe place and the dynamics have helped me grow.

My dream that night was of me going across the field in

sandals and avoiding the dog poo – a big improvement from drowning in mud.

A young woman on another retreat got into conversation with me. We were both supposed to be in silence, and at first, I was annoyed that she'd started a conversation. However, I relaxed into it and went with it. She too had been rejected by the Church of England selectors for ordination and found my story helpful and inspiring. She told me she'd been raped, and also said what she thought the statistics were. I said that my first selection conference left me feeling as though I'd been raped.

When I wrote in my journal, I wondered if I had remembered correctly that she said one in four women have been raped. Perhaps it was one in twenty. Maybe it was one in four women have experienced unwanted sexual contact. Later, when I checked it out, I found it was one in 200. Nevertheless, this is just reported rapes. The real figure will be much higher. It also depends upon how you define rape.

I also wrote the following: one in twenty women have been raped! Stripped, ripped apart, soul laid bare. Layer upon layer of grime and soil scrubbed away till flesh red and raw, throbbing in pain is exposed for all to see the inner state of me. Where is the ointment, the 'magic cream' that mothers use to sooth our wounds? If only it were so simple to soothe and remove the deep wounds on my soul.

The Time to Change campaign for mental health has the quote from Ruby Wax: "One in five people have dandruff. One in four people have mental health problems. I've had both." And I consider: Head & Shoulders cleared up my dandruff. Duloxetine has raised my mood. If only it were that easy to shift the blame, the shame. It's Time To Change – but how?

I have since been helped when someone I know well told me she'd been raped and she told me in such a matter-of-fact way that it helped me to accept what had happened to me wasn't so unusual. It 'normalised' it. What an awful thought, that rape can be 'normal'! Keeping silent only perpetuates the shame and need for silence on the part of the victims. However, I have found that it's only been in talking about it that I've been able to find peace and healing, including forgiving myself. For years I blamed myself for being drunk and stupid, for letting myself be vulnerable and then not having the maturity to know how to get myself out of it when my 'no' was ignored. And even now, I wonder if it is right to include so much detail in this story.

Although I was not a young child, being raped at about seventeen having started a sexual relationship at fifteen in a culture that had taboos surrounding sex and, rightly, rules to protect the young, I have had reactions similar to those who are sexually abused. I haven't suffered as badly as those who have been abused as young children by people who were trusted adults, but nevertheless, it had an impact that has taken years to counteract.

Monday: *Tortilla Soup*.[14] This film with noisy family scenes prompts me to think that I want to be part of a family, I want fun and I want to release repressed emotions. I also do not want to fear conflict. I experience an enormous step forward in my self-esteem at the group sharing. I spoke about the way that the other woman and I had conflicted the day before in a calm and sensitive way. She thanked me for speaking that way and I felt proud of myself.

I felt that I had got to the centre of what God was doing in me on the retreat. I decide that the next day I will make a Thank

You card for each of the group members and think of what to thank them for.

I did a painting entitled *And Can it Be*? It's based on my favourite hymn and shows my heart, still with bruises and scars, but nevertheless healed, and I am set free from the fears that bind me. The chains are broken.

I am able to add the final sixth impossible thing I believe: "I <u>can</u> give and receive love, with feeling, not just as a cold fact."

I left the retreat with a sense of a new chapter opening up for me. I had painted a picture of a muddy field with a fence at the end of it, without a gate. Beyond the fence is another field that is brighter. How could I get to the brighter field? I wrote the following summary of the retreat:

"Somewhere beyond your sense of right and wrong there is a bright field. Come and join me there." This was God's invitation to me. And I accepted but how was I to get there? Fenced off and no gate; I gazed across the field but got stuck in the mud, up to my neck, drowning. I'd gone on the retreat to rest, to regain strength. I was going to go with the flow, too tired to pray, too drained to think, not realising I was on the brink of a roller-coaster ride through rapids. Through films, dreams and new friends I faced the dragon of fear. Alone, only I could slay it. But before I could draw my sword, the battle plan, half formed, changed. Instead of slaying Fear, I would tame it. So riding my new friend, flying through the air above mud and mire, through laughter and tears till finally over the fence I came to rest in that bright field; at peace, quiet and still – still enough to know I am loved by God, by friends, by me."

Upon return from the retreat, I continued with a course of professional counselling, including talking about my attitude to sex. I was told that I was going through Jung's individuation process. I needed to accept my humanity and not expect perfection. During August I was again feeling very low and prayer had become something I do because I should and it lacked any real depth. I resolved to deepen my relationship with God.

Whilst awake and crying in the night, at three a.m. on 19th August 2010 I got up and did a painting of myself kneeling naked in a dark room with a bright light on my back. In order to try and connect with my inner child I stilled and quieted myself looking at the painting. I wrote the conversation at the same time as speaking partly so that I could remember anything significant, and also, I find writing can help. I wonder how the exercise would have gone had I just spoken. Writing slows down the thought process, makes what you say more concrete.

This is the conversation –

"Oh, Lizzy, my inner child. Naked, alone, crying in the night. What's wrong? Why won't you get up? What do you fear? Can't you feel the Light on your back? Warming you, bringing comfort and strength. He's always been there for you and with you. Such sorrow and despair when there's nobody there to care. But there is if you would but let them. Let them in. Let me in to help, to comfort, to love. Does a chrysalis fear being a butterfly? Is the process painful? Speak to me. I'll try to listen.

The reply I got was: "You don't care; not really. You just say you do. It's safe here in the dark where no one can see me." To which I said: "Is that really what you think? That I don't care?" And my inner child replied: "Yes, I do. You use me and abuse me. YOU JUST DON'T CARE"

This was not going well and I ended it by writing to

myself: "Look Liz – I'm getting cross with you now. You're trying my patience. I feel like taking you by the shoulders and giving you a good shake!"

I felt annoyed that the exercise hasn't worked – no great reconciliation, just acknowledgement once again that I don't like myself and wish I were dead with my inner parent just wanting to get back to work so I can be appreciated for what I do rather than for who I am. I question the depth of my prayer life and relationship with God, my struggles with the regular pattern of prayer and even question yet again whether God made a mistake in calling me. I don't feel I deserve the title Reverend. I then write the following:

"O God, here I am again, crying in the night, hiding from Your light, feeling the pain. Rescue me from despair, heal me deep within, help me to uncurl, to stand up and embrace Your light. I feel it on my back and am comforted but still afraid of who I am. Still not wanting to be me. Help me God. Help me please to trust, to believe, to accept that I am worthy of love and to want to be me. O God help me once again. Bring me up out of this dark pit to stand bathed in Love, enfolded in acceptance, enjoying being me."

In the days that follow I listen to a radio programme about abuse recovery. The website www.intothelight.org.uk is an organisation for survivors of childhood abuse and I recognise myself in some of the definitions. I am confused – had I been abused or not? I felt I was both victim and perpetrator. I have abused my inner child.

The counsellor I was seeing agrees that I can see my spiritual director for confession. She works with Jung's ideas of Persona and Shadow, suggesting that I get in touch with my Shadow, the sexy side of me. I want to forgive myself; I want my inner child to forgive me. At Holy Communion the

Beatitudes speak to me. I am blessed now as I'm in this mess. God's grace is at work in me. I come to see that circumstances – the Trail of Tragedy – has abused me. I pray through some prayers in a book for healing of sexuality.

I am nearly there

On Monday 30th August I awake slowly and realise that I do love myself: Today, I'm having a good day. I love myself – all of me. I am good; I am glad. I am <u>not</u> bad. I'm turning a corner, nearly there – not far to go. I feel as though I am emerging, slowly, carefully and like a beautiful butterfly, with gossamer wings of many colours.

I imagine myself on a shell, like Venus. When I paint it, I dress myself in a sexy purple gown and add on rainbow-coloured wings as a reminder of God's promises. Two months later I was enjoying preparing to go on a cruise– on my own. It was a brave step to go on holiday on my own and I felt that within the confines of a ship I might be safer than on land. I wanted to have a good time which included dancing as I'd been having ballroom and Latin dance lessons since the beginning of the year. I tried on various dresses to borrow from a friend. One of them just happened to be purple, with a side slit! Near enough like the one I painted myself in to give me a bit of a thrill and encouragement that God was with me.

By September I was almost off medication and returned to work full time. I didn't need any more time off and have not had any relapse since then. There were still some low times; tears were shed as I worked through the grief of a marriage that died. I was well enough to start looking for another job in 2011 and in June I moved to another parish. One job, one focus, a fresh start!

CHAPTER 11
I Become a Divorcee and Find Love Again

In 2012 I became a divorcee and my grieving continued. However, I did feel in the right frame of mind to think about the possibility of having another man in my life. I wanted to experience dating again – after all I had never actually dated a man as my dating years were all teenage ones. So with fear and trepidation I went onto a Christian dating website and after a few dates with one man that didn't go anywhere I got 'first contact' from a man on my birthday, which was a lovely gift to receive. We eventually went on a date and very quickly fell in love. I prayed about whether this was right for me and felt God's confirmation.

I attended a weekend retreat for separated and divorced people in October 2012 and was able, in that safe place, to work through grief and guilt. I was also able to understand that according to Roman Catholic rules I would have probably been granted an annulment due to the circumstances around my entering the marriage and our young ages. I felt I needed to hear that as I wanted release from the vows. Reflecting on this later though I came to see that it was a smokescreen and relinquishing responsibility away from self. I was probably still judging myself and finding myself guilty.

Several words of scripture spoke to me:

"I have loved you with an everlasting love; I have drawn you with unfailing kindness...

"I will build you up again," Jeremiah 31:3–4.

"There is a time for everything... a time to weep and a time to laugh, a time to mourn and a time to dance," Ecclesiastes 3:1–4.

"The Lord your God is with you... he will take great delight in you; in His love he will no longer rebuke you, but will rejoice over you with singing." Zephaniah 3:17.

I felt ready to move on and that this was a time for seeing God's promises of renewal and rebuilding come to fruition. During the weekend I was able to complete an exercise of listing ten positive things about myself that other people would say about me. I was very pleased to be able to do it with virtually no hesitation: a great step forward!

I felt at peace with myself and with my situation. The marriage that I was ill prepared for and that I would not have entered into if I hadn't been raped and in my right emotional state died several years ago. I had kept it going out of a sense of guilt and duty. The fact that I brought it to an end was a result of me following God's guidance as I understood it and of being healed emotionally and growing intellectually. It was the right thing to do. I wrote the following at the end of the weekend:

"There is now no condemnation for those who are in Christ Jesus our Lord." (Romans 8:1)

The past is gone. I live in the glory of God, washed in the blood of the Lamb: bright shining as a star; forgiven and free. My heart is free: free from vows I couldn't keep; free from sin's effects; free to love another.

For everything there is a season: a time for juvenile love

and mistakes – we all make them; a time for making the best of the situation we find ourselves in; a time for admitting we can't continue; a time for death and mourning; a time for starting to heal; a time for singing and rejoicing again in the freedom of loving being me. And that time is now.

I'm reminded of a Graham Kendrick song: *Such Love*. God weeps for the pain I've known. His love is filling me afresh, giving me hope, overflowing in joy, grace and love. I feel thankful for the good that came from the marriage. Rather than a funeral (which I had in 2009) I want a memorial. I don't now feel the need to be released from vows. It wasn't a marriage made in heaven, but neither was it hell, for there were moments of glory as well. We were a mismatched pair, probably incapable of becoming one in true love of body, mind and soul. We did our best with what we'd got and who we were. We created a secure safe home for two well-adjusted beautiful girls. But underneath the external happy home was deep unhappiness and increasing stress of trying to do the impossible. I'm thankful for the good times, the happiness and joy and even the humdrum day-to-day ordinariness. I'm sad it died and grieve for the dreamt-of 'happy ever after'. I'm glad I had the strength to declare it dead, to walk away and refuse to live a lie.

And now I'm free – free of guilt, pressure, failure, depression. I'm free of he who captured my heart and broke it. I'm free to be me: beautiful, loving, intelligent and creative. I'm free to become whoever and whatever God intends in the plans He has for me, to prosper me and not to harm for He has given me a hope and a future.

The retreat had ended, and there was a line drawn underneath the marriage. I was ready, willing and able to move on into whatever God had for me.

I married in May 2013 and since then there has been no sign of depression returning, despite there being some stressful times at work. It has been a long journey and I have no way of knowing that I will not suffer depression again in the future. But I am confident that the underlying cause of propensity towards depression has been healed. I know that I have a tendency towards depression when stressed and have learnt how to have a healthier balance of life in all its aspects. I believe that I HAVE recovered.

Are we there yet? Yes, we are!

EPILOGUE

At a weekend Life Stories retreat in January 2018 that seemed to be exactly the right timing for me during the sabbatical to finish writing this book, we were asked to reflect on our lives as if they were a river. We were to consider the life scripts (the ideas we have about ourselves and the world that we internalise when young), the narratives in our lives, the mix of dark and light… and let's face it much of life is mundane and ordinary. What were the stepping stones and stumbling blocks, detours and mistakes; the things that have made me who I am? This Ignatian exercise is well worth doing and one that I found easy as I had already done much of the work. I drew a river and in it were various twists and turns, as you would expect. I also did three waterfalls. Two of those were times when I felt I had no control over circumstances – the time I was raped and the car crash. However, the third was different. It was when I finally ended the marriage and we separated. I had had control then, but it was still traumatic and scary. So I changed it to rapids.

The next day we were asked to bring to the group two 'champagne moments' from our lives: one major, one not so big. Initially I found this difficult. I wanted to avoid the obvious wedding, childbirth, graduation and ordination events.

Looking at the picture I'd drawn what stood out were the

waterfalls. I am glad to be me, the person I am now and I wouldn't be me if I hadn't been raped or had the car crash that then cleared the way for ordination. I didn't want to drink champagne to the divorce as that seems wrong. But how can I drink champagne to the man who took advantage of a teenager who had had too much to drink and wouldn't listen to my terrified, *no*? How can I drink champagne to the man who was distracted or fell asleep at the wheel of his transit van and drove head on into my car at sixty mph? And yet, in a way, I am glad for those times. It is strange to think that although I could easily forgive the driver, for years I had carried the guilt of the former very deep within. It was one of my 'if onlys' that I'd been carrying. I had forgiven the man and my boyfriend at the time who dumped me, and myself. This weekend I was able to rid myself of the 'if only I hadn't been dumped and hadn't got drunk and been stupid' and say, 'yes I drink champagne to those two waterfalls because they have made me who I am today'.

The other champagne moment I chose to share was when I made a coat. In the first year of secondary school, we had to sew a domestic science apron using industrial nylon (it frayed like mad). It took all year as each step had to be presented to the teacher who invariably told me to do it again. She didn't like me (I thought) and made a different girl cry each week. When I did Duke of Edinburgh's Award, her disparaging comments on the report book were covered up and replaced by something more positive by the teacher in charge. So, this gave me a life script of not being very good at needlework. However when my children were young and we didn't have much money I made many of their clothes and at one point even made myself a camel hair coat, which involved tailoring… SO

THERE, MRS X!!... I CAN SEW. That's a champagne moment of realising that I can do what I put my mind to.

I went back to the picture and added some colour. I allocated a different colour to each of my 'life scripts' that have been gradually redeemed and transformed over the years into a 'champagne moment'. With the addition of blue and indigo for the water they created a rainbow effect: a wonderful symbol of God's promises. These themes have been woven into my life and are part of the warp and weft, the light and dark that make the beautiful tapestry that is me.

The *"I can't sew"* script is clearly not true as I can sew and I have the making a coat champagne moment.

The *"I am stupid and thick, my brother is the clever one"* is not true. I spent too much time staring out of the window at junior school and failed the eleven plus and was sent to the secondary modern school whereas my older brother had passed and gone to the grammar school. At the time, apparently, I was upset because the uniform was better at the grammar school, having a brown blazer with golden braid. These formative events became registered within me as a life script of "I am stupid and thick, my brother is the clever one". This took some time to undo. Despite gaining very high secretarial qualifications that would entitle me to membership of the Institute of Qualified Private Secretaries and letters after my name, two A levels in my thirties and a BSc at forty-two (during which time I discovered that there was a cap on how many girls were allowed to go to the grammar school, so I may not have actually failed the eleven plus as there may have simply been too many girls who had), when I went to theological college and studied for Master of Theology I still thought I was thick. I had a few weeks of counselling to overcome my inferiority complex. There was a wonderful moment sometime after I graduated when I realised that the academic hood I could now wear was golden in colour – far more gold and of more standing than that on the blazer I had so wanted to wear. Getting an MTh is very definitely a champagne moment.

The *"I'm a naughty disobedient girl, undeserving and mummy doesn't love me"* is mainly based on what I call the yellow dress incident. My cousin had been a bridesmaid and I got her yellow dress handed down to wear for parities. I was possibly about five or six years old. One day I went to a friend's birthday party down the road wearing the yellow dress and instead of going home afterwards to get changed as I'd been told I went out to play. I may or may not have got the dress dirty, I don't remember, but I do remember having a good, old-fashioned, over the knee spanking on my bare bottom, for not going home when I'd been told to. I don't know what else happened in my young years but I was left with the feeling that Mummy didn't love me and that I was a naughty girl. My relationship with my mother wasn't good in my teenage years but improved when I had children. Nevertheless, when she died, what I needed most and now could not have, was to hear her say she loved me. I had always been more of a Daddy's girl, able to twist him around my little finger. After her death my dad showed more love and affection than ever before and we would often say 'I love you'. I really did drink champagne when I wore my white wedding dress and became Mrs Jones.

The *"I'm only a girl so can't be what I want (i.e. accountant like my dad)"* was transformed – women CAN be ordained – and I was and I think we did drink champagne.

And finally, the *"I can't draw or paint"* is clearly not true as I am proving. I can learn and develop – I am creative. Let's put a bottle in the fridge!

Writing this book has challenged me. Dare I let people see my 'art' on the accompanying pdf available on my website? It isn't very good – but having started a blog and posted some pictures online on various Facebook groups I've been encouraged and surprised that people have said they like my art. Dare I let people know some of the very personal things? Will anyone want to read it? I have got to the point of not needing to do it for my own healing… praise God: that is done. But I do want to encourage others to risk taking their own journey of faith, of letting down the barriers and letting God in to heal and transform their negative voices.

I will continue with the art and play with paint as often as I can, not worrying about getting my dress dirty, not worrying about mistakes – after all, that's how we learn. When I went for a walk on the Life Stories Retreat, down to the river, and I heard the waterfall at the weir I was drawn to stop and look. I had got to where I needed to be on that walk. I sensed God say that the waterfalls were key. Not just for my champagne moments, but for my creativity. Being creative needs energy, plus time and space. Energy comes from movement, be that water or wind. The first two of my waterfalls were times when I had no control, which is why they were so traumatic. The third waterfall was a time when I did have an element of control, or steering the course, which is why I changed it to rapids. I sensed God say that the Holy Spirit, the wind of God, will be the energy for being creative. Whenever I've been creative in the past (other than on retreats) it has been following a pattern or instructions (e.g. knitting, sewing, decorating special birthday cakes). I need someone to tell me what to do. God will inspire me. So I shouldn't worry about what to do. He will guide me. All I need to do is ensure I make time and space in my busy schedule. If this is something He wants me to do – and I believe it is and that it will play some part in ministry in the future (perhaps when I retire) – then I should give it a higher priority than at present. Being creative is just as valid a use of time as serious theological reading.

[1]*Lord you put a new song in my mouth*© Ears & Eyes Music 1985

[2]*Such Love* by Graham Kendrick© 1988 Make Way Music

[3]*Be Bold, Be Strong*. Words and Music © 1984 Word Music, LLC(Admin. by Song Solutions CopyCare, 14 Horsted Square, Uckfield, East Sussex, TN22 1QG.

[4]*Be Still, for the Presence of the Lord*. Words: David J. Evans (b. 1957) Copyright © 1986 Thankyou Music (Admin. by kingswaysongs.com).

[5]*Suscipe* is the Latin word for 'receive.' While it is often mistakenly identified as having its origins as the title of a prayer written by St Ignatius of Loyola, founder of the Society of Jesus, in the early sixteenth century incorporated into the *Spiritual Exercises of Ignatius of Loyola*, the Suscipe actually has a prior origin going back to monastic profession, in reciting Psalm 118. Ignatius relies on this prior tradition. This article in its present state focuses mainly on Ignatius' Suscipe prayer.

Ignatius wrote that the 'spiritual exercises' is the name given to every way of preparing and disposing one's soul to rid oneself of all disordered attachments, so that once rid of them one might seek and find the divine will in regard to the disposition of one's life for the good of the soul. The Exercises are a set of meditations, prayers, and mental exercises to be carried out over a four-week time period, most appropriately on a secluded retreat.

Context of Ignatius' Suscipe

The Suscipe is not found in any of the four weeks of the Spiritual Exercises, but rather was included by Ignatius as additional material in regard to the "contemplation for attaining love" at the end of the Exercises. In this section, Ignatius speaks of the immeasurable love of God that is bestowed upon all of creation, and then asks what he might offer to such a loving God:

First Point. This is to recall to mind the blessings of creation and redemption, and the special favors I have received.

I will ponder with great affection how much God our Lord has done for me, and how much He has given me of what He possesses, and finally, how much, as far as He can, the same Lord desires to give Himself to me according to His divine decrees.

Then I will reflect upon myself, and consider, according to all reason and justice, what I ought to offer the Divine Majesty, that is, all I possess and myself with it. Thus, as one would who is moved by great feeling, I will make this offering of myself:

'Receive, O Lord, all my liberty. Take my memory, my understanding, and my entire will. Whatsoever I have or hold, You have given me; I give it all back to You and surrender it wholly to be governed by your will. Give me only your love and your grace, and I am rich enough and ask for nothing more.' (Spiritual Exercises, #234)

from http://en.wikipedia.org/wiki/Suscipe

[6]*Memories of Bliss: God, Sex and Us* by Jo Ind, page 74

[7] From common worship psalter© The Archbishops' Council of the Church of England.

[8]*Julie & Julia* is a 2009 American comedy-drama film written and directed by Nora Ephron starring Meryl Streep, Amy Adams, Stanley Tucci, and Chris Messina. The film contrasts the life of chef Julia Child in the early years of her culinary career with the life of young New Yorker Julie Powell, who aspires to cook all 524 recipes in Child's cookbook in 365 days, a challenge she described on her popular blog that made her a published author.[2]

[9]*Crouching Tiger, Hidden Dragon*, 2000. This is the story of two women, both capable fighters, whose fates intertwine during the Ching Dynasty. One of them tries passionately to break free from the constraint society has placed upon her, even if it means giving up her aristocratic privileges for a life of crime and passion. The other, in her lifelong pursuit of justice and honour, only too late discovers the consequences of unfulfilled love. Their two destinies will lead them to a violent and astonishing showdown, in which each will make a surprising, climatic choice.

[10]*Man on Wire* is a 2008 British biographical documentary film directed by James Marsh. The film chronicles Philippe Petit's 1974 high-wire walk between the Twin Towers of New York's World Trade Center.

[11]*The Water Horse.*When a lonely young boy named Angus discovers a large, mysterious egg along the shores of Loch Ness, no one is prepared for what lies within. He soon discovers that the strange, mischievous hatchling inside is none other than the Water Horse, the loch's most mysterious and fabled creature! But with the Water Horse growing ten times its size every day, Angus finds it increasingly difficult to keep his new friend a secret.

[12]*Philadelphia.* Fearing it would compromise his career, lawyer Andrew Beckett (Tom Hanks) hides his homosexuality and HIV status at a powerful Philadelphia law firm. But his secret is exposed when a colleague spots the illness's telltale lesions. Fired shortly afterwards, Beckett resolves to sue for discrimination, teaming up with Joe Miller (Denzel Washington), the only

lawyer willing to help. In court, they face one of his ex-employer's top litigators, Belinda Conine (Mary Steenburgen). Release date: 25 February 1994.

[13]*The Postman.* A true cinema delight for romantics and lovers of enriched drama, *Il Postino – The Postman* is a gentle Italian tale about the power of words, the strength of love and the ability to overcome life's many emotional challenges. Mario (Massimo Troisi) is a newly appointed mailman who is madly in love with the most beautiful woman in town, Beatrice Russo (Maria Grazia Cucinotta). Bumbling, interminably shy and far too nervous to tell her how he feels, Mario becomes inspired when a world-famous Chilean poet visits the small island community. Pablo Neruda (Philippe Noiret) is a revelation to the otherwise introverted and soft-spoken Mario and with his expert help Mario not only finds the right words to woo Beatrice but has a fighting chance to win her over.

[14]*Tortilla Soup.* Maria Ripoli's remake of Ang Lee's film *Eat Drink Man Woman* has the action taking place within an Hispanic-American family living in California. Gourmet chef (Héctor Elizondo) finds that his sense of taste is diminishing with age but still manages to get his three (unmarried) daughters around the dinner table regularly along with various guests. His eldest, Letitia (Elizabeth Peña) is a repressed school-teacher, his middle daughter, Carmen (Jacqueline Obradors) has just accepted the offer of a new job in Barcelona (much to the displeasure of her father), and his youngest, Maribel (Tamara Mello) has set her eyes on a handsome Brazilian student (Nikolai Kinski). Amongst the various guests are a shy single mother, her overpowering mother (Raquel Welch) and a ballplayer to whom Letitia's students have been secretly sending love letters from her.